McGraw-Hill

Introduction to Psychology Practice Tests

R. Eric Landrum
Boise State University

McGraw-Hill College

Boston   Burr Ridge, IL   Dubuque, IA   Madison, WI   New York   San Francisco   St. Louis
Bangkok   Bogotá   Caracas   Lisbon   London   Madrid
Mexico City   Milan   New Delhi   Seoul   Singapore   Sydney   Taipei   Toronto

McGraw-Hill College

A Division of The McGraw·Hill Companies

MCGRAW-HILL INTRODUCTION TO PSYCHOLOGY PRACTICE TESTS

9 BKM BKM   9 0 9 8 7 6 5 4 3 2 1 0

ISBN 0-07-229694-1

www.mhhe.com

CONTENTS

INTRODUCTION

These multiple-choice practice tests have been compiled to give you a glimpse of the type of test questions you may encounter on the material covered in an Introduction to Psychology course. The practice tests provide a sample of the types of questions that often appear on exams.

Each chapter begins with a list of learning objectives. You can use the learning objectives in various ways. For example, you can read the objectives before reading the chapter to get an overview of the topics that you will be reading about in the book. While reading, pay attention to the terms, concepts, names, and ideas mentioned in the objectives. Also, after you have read the chapter, check your understanding of the textbook by attempting to fulfill the learning objectives. If something in an objective seems unclear, you may wish to re-read that portion of the chapter.

The sample multiple-choice questions are similar to the type you might be asked to respond to by your instructor. There are <u>two</u> questions per objective. Answering the question correctly for a given learning objective does not necessarily guarantee a full understanding of the concepts expressed by the objective. On the other hand, if you answer the question incorrectly, it could signal that you need to return to that section of the chapter for more study.

Using the practice tests and the learning objectives can help you master the material in your textbook, but you should note that it is doubtful that your instructor will use these exact same items for an actual test. You need to review your class notes, the textbook, and the learning objectives before any exam. For some excellent tips on improving your performance in class, see your textbook. For additional review, there may be a *Student Study Guide* available for your particular textbook. Your instructor or bookstore can order the study guide if it is not already available in your bookstore.

Good luck!

1 THE SCIENCE & SCOPE OF PSYCHOLOGY

LEARNING OBJECTIVES

1.	Describe Aristotle's role in the history of psychology and understand the definition of psychology.
2.	Identify and define the four goals of psychology.
3.	Identify and compare early views of psychology that focused on the elements of conscious experience, including Wundt, Titchener, the Structuralists, Alston, and the Gestalt psychologists.
4.	Identify and compare views in psychology that focused on the functions of the conscious mind, including James, the Functionalists, Ebbinghaus, Calkins, and Binet. Also, explain functionalism's influence on contemporary psychology, namely cognition.
5.	Describe the origins of behaviorism and social learning theory.
6.	Identify the early views of psychology that focused on the nature of the unconscious mind.
7.	Describe the biological and sociocultural perspectives and explain their influence on contemporary psychology.
8.	Identify and define the terms associated with the sociocultural perspective.
9.	Describe how sociocultural factors influenced the history of psychology.
10.	Describe the differences between basic and applied areas of psychology; list and describe examples of both areas.
11.	Describe the relationship between psychology and psychiatry.
12.	Identify the requirements necessary for the use of the scientific method in psychology.
13.	Recognize three descriptive methods used in psychology and understand how they are used.
14.	Know the goal of the correlational method and understand how it is used.
15.	Understand how and when formal experiments are used.
16.	Distinguish between a dependent and an independent variable; distinguish between a control group and an experimental group.
17.	List and define the five major ethical principles of research with human participants.
18.	Understand why psychologists use animals in research and describe the ethical principles associated with animal studies.
19.	Identify the beliefs commonly shared by psychologists about human nature and behavior.

SAMPLE QUESTIONS

1. Psychology is best defined as the science of
   a. thought and emotion.
   b. behavior and mental processes.
   c. observation and description.
   d. knowledge acquisition.

2. The essential difference between behavior and mental processes is
   a. complexity.
   b. observability.
   c. controllability.
   d. ease of description.

3. Which of the following is <u>NOT</u> a goal of psychology?
   a. to control
   b. to understand
   c. to influence
   d. to describe

4. If you were using a survey to gather information about people, which goal of psychology would you be attempting?
   a. describe
   b. hypothesize
   c. influence
   d. predict

5. When did psychology became a recognized field of study?
   a. about 200 years ago when introduced by Aristotle
   b. when introduced in Greece around the year 384 B.C
   c. in the late 1800s when the first laboratory was established
   d. soon after philosophers converted to biological studies

6. Of the following experimental situations, which would most likely be conducted by a structuralist?
   a. documenting subject's descriptions of an experience
   b. asking subjects to remember a list of words
   c. testing rats in a maze to see how fast they learn
   d. rewarding subjects for solving problems

7. Functionalists would agree that the human mind
   a. evolved to promote survival.
   b. cannot be studied by man.
   c. can be isolated into basic elements.
   d. is best studied by introspection.

8. William James was highly influential in the development of the school of thought in psychology known as
   a. psychoanalysis.
   b. Gestalt psychology.
   c. structuralism.
   d. functionalism.

9. The ideas of Pavlov and Watson influenced the school of thought known as
   a. behaviorism.
   b. psychoanalysis.
   c. structuralism.
   d. Gestalt psychology.

10. The emphasis of behaviorism is on
    a. mental elements.
    b. unconscious thoughts.
    c. perceptual relationships.
    d. observable events.

11. Which school of psychology was founded and developed by Sigmund Freud?
    a. behaviorism
    b. humanism
    c. psychoanalysis
    d. Gestalt psychology

12. What differentiated Sigmund Freud from most of the other influential founders of psychology?
    a. Freud was the only founder from a European country.
    b. Freud was trained as a philosopher and teacher.
    c. Freud was not interested in the unconscious mind.
    d. Freud was a physician and treated psychological problems.

13. You are told that Dr. X researches the behavior patterns of a group of French descendants who live near the mouth of the Mississippi River. Dr. X is most likely a
    a. humanistic psychologist.
    b. biological psychologist.
    c. cognitive psychologist.
    d. sociocultural psychologist.

14. A psychologist who studies the role the brain plays in psychological processes uses which approach?
    a. biological perspective
    b. cognitive perspective
    c. humanistic viewpoint
    d. sociocultural viewpoint

15. Gender identity and ethnic identity are topics that are of most importance to
    a. biological psychologists.
    b. sociocultural psychologists.
    c. humanistic psychologists.
    d. Gestalt psychologists.

16. The patterns of behavior, beliefs, and values that are shared by a group of people defines
    a. society.
    b. gender identity.
    c. culture.
    d. ethnicity.

17. One reason that men greatly outnumbered women in the early history of psychology was that
    a. the early topics in psychology were of interest only to men.
    b. women could work only when they had supplemental income.
    c. most women in psychology went into teaching.
    d. institutions discriminated against women.

18.   Women who had successful careers in psychology at the beginning of the 20th century for the most part
        a.   were not married.
        b.   did not do research.
        c.   worked alone.
        d.   were therapists.

19.   The specialty in the basic experimental area that emphasizes reasoning, thinking, and the mental processes
        associated with perception, language, and problem solving is
        a.   sociocultural psychology.
        b.   psychoanalysis.
        c.   cognitive psychology.
        d.   social learning theory.

20.   Modern psychology can be roughly divided into _____ fields.
        a.   cognitive and experimental
        b.   educational and experimental
        c.   basic and applied
        d.   experimental and basic

21.   In general, a clinical psychologist would hold a(n) _____ degree.
        a.   M.D.
        b.   Ph.D.
        c.   B.A.
        d.   M.S.

22.   What is the major difference between psychologists and psychiatrists?
        a.   psychologists treat more severe mental problems
        b.   psychiatrists are medical doctors
        c.   psychologists have a doctoral degree
        d.   psychiatrists do not use drug treatments

23.   In order for human behavior to be studied by science, psychologists must believe that human behavior is
        a.   not determined.
        b.   random.
        c.   predictable.
        d.   universal.

24.   What assumption about human behavior is necessary for a scientific psychology?
        a.   Human nature is basically good.
        b.   Human beings are rational creatures.
        c.   Human behavior is predictable.
        d.   Human behavior is disorderly.

25.   The descriptive methods used in psychology may best be described as
        a.   not very scientific methods.
        b.   the simplest scientific methods.
        c.   the method used most by behaviorists.
        d.   the most controlled scientific method.

26.   What do the survey technique and naturalistic observation have in common?
        a.   They are both descriptive research methods.
        b.   They are both experimental research methods.
        c.   They both produce a coefficient of correlation.
        d.   They both contain a control group and a treatment group.

27. Prediction is the goal of which research method?
    a. correlational
    b. formal experiment
    c. descriptive
    d. clinical

28. A research study reported a relationship between amount of sleep and job performance. Which research method did the researchers use?
    a. survey
    b. clinical
    c. industrial
    d. correlational

29. What is the primary goal of the formal experiment?
    a. to predict behavior
    b. to understand behavior
    c. to describe behavior
    d. to control behavior

30. Which of the following research techniques allows fairly confident conclusions about cause-and-effect relationships?
    a. case study
    b. correlational research
    c. descriptive survey
    d. formal experiment

31. In a formal experiment, the variable that the experimenter wants to measure is called the _____ variable.
    a. independent
    b. dependent
    c. basic
    d. control

32. A psychologist is studying the effect of varying levels of caffeine on anxiety. In this experiment, caffeine level is the
    a. correlation coefficient.
    b. dependent variable.
    c. independent variable.
    d. uncontrolled variable.

33. Dr. X required all his students without exception to participate in an experiment for part of the course grade. What is true regarding Dr. X's use of the ethical principles of human research?
    a. He does not need to use informed consent.
    b. He is violating freedom from coercion.
    c. He is violating the use of deception.
    d. He will not be required to use debriefing.

34. The American Psychological Association has established a set of ethical principles for research with human participants. The experimenter is usually required to give participants a complete description of the experiment before they are allowed to participate. This illustrates the principle of
    a. debriefing.
    b. informed consent.
    c. freedom from coercion.
    d. indoctrination.

35. Which of the following is not part of the ethical guidelines of research with animals?
    a. necessity
    b. freedom from coercion
    c. healthy care of animals
    d. humane treatment

36. What is meant by the ethical principle called necessity?
    a. Human subjects must be informed about research outcomes only if necessary.
    b. Researchers should never deprive animal subjects from basic needs.
    c. It is necessary that researchers treat animals just like human subjects.
    d. Animals should be used in studies only if it increases our understanding of behavior.

37. What do we know to be true about human behavior?
    a. Humans are social animals.
    b. People do not have free will.
    c. It can only be understood by psychologists.

38. Because humans work to feed, shelter, and clothe themselves, we know that human behavior is
    a. motivated.
    b. maladaptive.
    c. selfish.
    d. simplistic.

Chapter 1 Answer Key

1. b	6. a	11. c	16. c	21. b	26. a	31. b	36. d
2. b	7. a	12. d	17. d	22. b	27. a	32. c	37. a
3. a	8. d	13. d	18. a	23. c	28. d	33. b	38. a
4. a	9. a	14. a	19. c	24. c	29. b	34. b	
5. c	10. d	15. b	20. c	25. b	30. d	35. b	

2 BIOLOGICAL FOUNDATIONS: BRAIN & BEHAVIOR

LEARNING OBJECTIVES

1. Understand the importance of the neuron and differentiate among the neuron's cell body, dendrite, and axon.
2. Summarize the processes of neural transmission and synaptic transmission.
3. Differentiate the central nervous system from the peripheral nervous system and explain the differences among afferent neurons, efferent neurons, and interneurons.
4. List the functions of the somatic and autonomic nervous systems and describe the roles of the sympathetic and parasympathetic divisions of the autonomic nervous system.
5. Describe the techniques that provide images of the brain and brain functions.
6. List the three major divisions of the brain and know their subcomponents.
7. Explain the basic functions of the hindbrain and midbrain.
8. Summarize the functions of the regions of the forebrain, specifically the thalamus, hypothalamus, limbic system, and cerebral cortex.
9. Identify the location and functions of the four lobes and the association areas of the cerebral cortex.
10. Explain how the two cerebral hemispheres communicate and describe the changes that occur if the corpus callosum is severed.
11. Discuss the role of the cerebral cortex in processing emotional information.
12. Identify examples of the brain acting as an interactive system and explain the differences between parallel and serial processing.
13. Identify the endocrine glands and understand how the endocrine system communicates and how it regulates body processes.
14. Identify the hormones related to each endocrine gland and understand their functions.
15. Know the relationship between genes and chromosomes and understand how dominant and recessive genes affect physical and behavioral traits.
16. Summarize the role of twin studies and adoption studies in genetic research.
17. Understand inheritance in terms of its influence on personality development and abnormal behavior.

SAMPLE QUESTIONS

1. The basic unit of the nervous system is called the
   a. nerve.
   b. brain.
   c. synapse.
   d. neuron.

2. Approximately, how many neurons compose the human brain?
   a. 20 to 50 thousand
   b. 100 million
   c. 5 billion
   d. 100 billion

3. When a neuron is at rest, which ion is highly concentrated just outside the cell membrane?
   a. negative polarization ions
   b. positive neurotransmitters
   c. positive sodium ions
   d. negative potassium ions

4. The neuron cell membrane permits some substances to pass through but not others; this is because the membrane is
   a. depolarized.
   b. semipermeable.
   c. electrically charged.
   d. covered with myelin.

5. Input is to output as
   a. inhibitory substance is to excitatory substance.
   b. peripheral nervous system is to afferent neurons.
   c. afferent neuron is to efferent neuron.
   d. association neuron is to peripheral nervous system.

6. Where are interneurons located?
   a. between afferent and efferent neurons
   b. between dendrites and axons
   c. between muscles and efferent neurons
   d. between synaptic knobs and dendrites

7. A polygraph can monitor changes in heart rate, breathing, and sweating. What part of the nervous system does it monitor?
   a. somatic
   b. afferent
   c. central
   d. autonomic

8. The division of the peripheral nervous system that plays a significant role in motivation and emotion is the
   a. autonomic division.
   b. somatic division.
   c. central division.
   d. association cortex.

9. To map the brain's electrical activity, a(n) _____ is used.
   a. EEG
   b. PET
   c. EMG
   d. MRI

10. Magnetic resonance imaging is a technique that works by
    a. measuring the rate at which brain cells use glucose.
    b. constructing a 3-dimensional image from X rays.
    c. transducing the electrical activity of individual neurons.
    d. detecting and interpreting magnetic activity from atomic nuclei.

11. What do the pons and medulla have in common?
    a. They are both parts of the hindbrain.
    b. They are both parts of the midbrain.
    c. They are both parts of the forebrain.
    d. They are both parts of the limbic system.

12. The thalamus and limbic system are parts of the
    a. forebrain.
    b. midbrain.
    c. cerebellum.
    d. medulla.

13. A paramedic arrives at an accident. One of the people injured has a problem breathing and cannot stand upright. Most likely, the area of the hindbrain damaged is the
    a. pons.
    b. medulla.
    c. cerebrum.
    d. thalamus.

14. If a person's cerebellum was damaged in an accident, you would expect the person to have a problem with
    a. breathing and heart rate.
    b. seeing and hearing.
    c. talking and understanding.
    d. balance and muscle coordination.

15. Which structure links the upper and lower centers of the brain?
    a. amygdala
    b. hippocampus
    c. thalamus
    d. hypothalamus

16. If there is such a thing as a "pleasure center" in the brain, it would most likely be located in the
    a. hypothalamus.
    b. basal ganglia.
    c. hindbrain.
    d. reticular formation.

17. Which of the following is one of the cerebral lobes of the brain?
    a. cerebellar
    b. patellar
    c. temporal
    d. medulla

18. How many cerebral lobes are in the human brain?
    a. six
    b. four
    c. three
    d. two

19. The cerebral cortex is made up of two nearly separate parts called the
    a. association areas.
    b. cerebellar lobes.
    c. cerebral hemispheres.
    d. cerebral callosum.

20. What is the name of the large bundle of axons that connect the two halves of the brain?
    a. basal ganglia
    b. cingulate gyrus
    c. hypothalamus
    d. corpus callosum

21. There is evidence that the left hemisphere is involved in processing _____, and the right hemisphere is involved in processing _____.
    a. positive emotions; negative emotions
    b. emotional reactions; abstract thought
    c. spatial information; complex language
    d. spoken language; language production

22. When the right hemisphere is damaged, people typically react with _____ emotions.
    a. normal
    b. depressed
    c. heightened
    d. elated

23. Intellectual and emotional functioning are commonly mediated
    a. by the left parietal lobe.
    b. through parallel types of processing.
    c. by the right parietal lobe.
    d. through serial types of processing.

24. In general, when the brain processes information it uses
    a. parallel processing.
    b. serial processing.
    c. conscious processing.
    d. localized processing.

25. The pituitary gland is primarily controlled by the
    a. thyroid.
    b. corpus callosum.
    c. hypothalamus.
    d. hippocampus.

26. Biological rhythms are regulated by which endocrine gland?
    a. pancreas
    b. pineal
    c. thyroid
    d. parathyroid

27. Melatonin is to cortisol as
   a. parathyroid is to pituitary.
   b. parathyroid is to thyroid.
   c. pineal is to adrenal.
   d. pineal is to thyroid.

28. An increase in epinephrine in the bloodstream causes a(n)
   a. increase in heart rate.
   b. drop in blood pressure.
   c. constriction of the pupils.
   d. slowing of respiration.

29. The human cell has how many pairs of chromosomes?
   a. 20
   b. 23
   c. 26
   d. 30

30. What differentiates a gamete from a zygote?
   a. location in the nervous system
   b. whether the chromosomes are paired
   c. type of hormone secreted
   d. length of axon

31. Twin studies and adoption studies are _____ of research.
   a. unrelated types
   b. not scientific methods
   c. descriptive methods
   d. experimental methods

32. Dizygotic twins are as genetically alike as
   a. other siblings.
   b. their parents.
   c. monozygotic twins.
   d. clones.

33. If a child has a parent with a major psychological disorder such as schizophrenia, the child has
   a. a 30 percent chance of developing the schizophrenia.
   b. just as much chance of developing schizophrenia as anyone.
   c. a 1 in 10 chance of developing schizophrenia.
   d. a 50 percent chance of developing schizophrenia.

34. Which of the following supports the idea that people can inherit a predisposition for schizophrenia?
   a. if one dizygotic twin has schizophrenia the other will too
   b. if a dizygotic twin has schizophrenia the other will about 50 percent of the time
   c. if a monozygotic twin has schizophrenia the other will about 50 percent of the time
   d. if a monozygotic twin has schizophrenia the other will too

Chapter 2 Answer Key

1. d	6. a	11. a	16. a	21. a	26. b	31. c
2. d	7. d	12. a	17. c	22. a	27. c	32. a
3. c	8. a	13. b	18. b	23. b	28. a	33. c
4. b	9. a	14. d	19. c	24. a	29. b	34. c
5. c	10. d	15. c	20. d	25. c	30. b	

3 SENSATION & PERCEPTION

LEARNING OBJECTIVES

1. Distinguish between sensation and perception and define sense organ, sensory receptor, and stimulus.
2. Define transduction.
3. Compare and contrast the absolute threshold and the difference threshold.
4. Understand sensory adaptation.
5. Define psychophysics and understand Weber's law.
6. Understand the nature of light.
7. Describe how the different parts of the eye work together to produce vision.
8. Describe the roles played by the rods and cones in both dark adaptation and light adaptation.
9. Compare and contrast the trichromatic theory and the opponent-process theory of color vision, describing the evidence for each.
10. Understand the nature of sound.
11. Explain how different parts of the ear work together to produce audition (hearing).
12. Describe the roles played by the vestibular organ and the kinesthetic receptors in providing information about orientation and movement.
13. List the four different general types of skin receptors and describe the three types of stimuli that can be detected by the skin.
14. Explain the gate control theory of pain and describe the role played by endorphins in "runners high," acupuncture, and placebos.
15. Define phantom limb pain and identify its possible causes.
16. List the four basic taste sensations and identify other factors that influence our perception of taste.
17. List the seven primary qualities of odors and explain the stereochemical theory.
18. Name and describe the five Gestalt principles of perceptual organization.
19. Describe the four kinds of perceptual constancy.
20. Identify the monocular cues and binocular cues of depth perception.
21. Distinguish between the visual illusions and describe how they are produced.
22. Identify how individual and cultural factors influence perception.

SAMPLE QUESTIONS

1. Sensory information is interpreted through the process of
    a. sensation.
    b. translation.
    c. perception.
    d. sensory adaptation.

2. The process of receiving, translating, and transmitting messages from the outside world to the brain is called
    a. sensation.
    b. selective attention.
    c. perception.
    d. cognition.

3. The process by which physical energy from the environment is converted to neural signals is
    a. perception.
    b. transduction.
    c. psychophysics.
    d. adaptation.

4. Where does the process of transduction take place?
    a. at the cortical level
    b. at the interneuron level
    c. at the receptor cell level
    d. at the spinal cord level

5. The point at which two stimuli are detected as different 50 percent of the time is known as the
    a. absolute threshold.
    b. difference threshold.
    c. opponent-process theory.
    d. adaptation point.

6. An architect is designing apartments and wants them to be soundproof. She asks a psychologist what the smallest amount of sound is that can be heard. Her question is most related to the
    a. absolute threshold.
    b. difference threshold.
    c. Weber's law.
    d. sensory receptors.

7. Sensory adaptation refers to
    a. the way that receptors adapt to the impact of being transduced.
    b. reduction in sensitivity resulting from repeated stimulation.
    c. the process of adapting sensations into perceptions.
    d. the increase in the difference threshold with time.

8. You are driving with the stereo set at what you believe to be a comfortable level. You stop to pick up your date who claims that the stereo is much too loud. The best explanation is
    a. your date does not like music.
    b. your date has more sensitive hearing.
    c. you had habituated to the loudness.
    d. you have reached your absolute threshold.

9. The area of investigation that studies the relationship between physical properties and psychological sensations is
   a. psychophysiology.
   b. sensory physiology.
   c. psychophysics.
   d. perception.

10. If a person wishes to study how vision is affected by various stimulus conditions, which specialty field within psychology would be BEST suited to his or her interest?
    a. environmental psychology
    b. sensory physiology
    c. psychophysics
    d. kinesthetics

11. A change in the wavelength of light would result in a change in
    a. brightness.
    b. saturation.
    c. hue.
    d. timbre.

12. Joe wants his research subjects to view a different pure color every 5 seconds. What should he do?
    a. Increase the intensity of light incrementally every 5 seconds.
    b. Start with a single wavelength of light and add a wavelength every 5 seconds.
    c. Show single wavelengths of various lengths every 5 seconds.
    d. Show varying forms of electromagnetic radiation every 5 seconds.

13. The major purpose of the iris is to
    a. protect the eye from injury.
    b. regulate the amount light entering the eye.
    c. focus light on the retina.
    d. transduce light energy.

14. The clear membrane just in front of the iris through which light first passes is the
    a. retina.
    b. lens.
    c. cornea.
    d. rod.

15. Night blindness can result from
    a. dark adaptation.
    b. vitamin A deficiency.
    c. weak cone vision.
    d. poor light adaptation.

16. Increases in the sensitivity of the eye in semi-darkness following an abrupt reduction in overall illumination is known as
    a. light adaptation.
    b. dark adaptation.
    c. opponent-process theory.
    d. wavelength blindness.

17. Trichromatic theory proposes that the human retina contains _____ different _____.
    a. 3; kinds of rods
    b. 3; kinds of cones
    c. 2; kinds of color receptors
    d. 2; complementary colors

18. Which theory of color vision accounts for the fact that you see a black spot after looking at a camera that has flashed?
    a. trichromatic
    b. monochromatic
    c. stereochemical
    d. opponent-process

19. We hear a tuning fork when it is struck because it
    a. electromagnetically stimulates the vestibular system.
    b. causes compression and rarefaction of air molecules.
    c. transduces air molecules into energy.
    d. causes the oval window to uncurl and recoil.

20. If you changed the frequency of the sound wave, you would probably change the
    a. timbre.
    b. intensity.
    c. pitch.
    d. loudness.

21. The outer part of the ear that helps collect sound is called the
    a. oval window.
    b. organ of Corti.
    c. stirrup.
    d. pinna.

22. The bones of the middle ear are set into motion by vibrations of the
    a. cochlea.
    b. eardrum.
    c. saccule.
    d. basilar membrane.

23. When conflicting messages are sent to the brain by the vestibular organs, we often experience
    a. euphoria.
    b. motion sickness.
    c. depression.
    d. conflict

24. With your eyes closed, touch the tip of your nose with your right index finger. You are able to do this mainly because of information from
    a. learned physical abilities.
    b. your vestibular sense.
    c. your kinesthetic sense.
    d. your skin senses.

25. The level of sensitivity of certain parts of the skin is controlled by the
    a. temperature of the surroundings.
    b. number of nerve cells in the area.
    c. level of arousal.
    d. thickness of the epidermis.

26. When you are feeling pain, which type of skin receptor is primarily involved?
    a. basket cells
    b. specialized end bulbs
    c. free nerve endings
    d. tactile discs

27. Pain signals are transmitted to the brain via
    a. multiple gates.
    b. the spinal cord.
    c. tactile discs.
    d. basket cells.

28. How does myelin influence the transmission of pain signals?
    a. slows the message
    b. speeds the message
    c. changes the message
    d. blocks the message

29. What percentage of amputees feel pain in their missing limbs?
    a. less than 5 percent
    b. about 17 percent
    c. less than 50 percent
    d. as many as 70 percent

30. What may persons with spinal cord damage have in common to persons who have lost an arm or leg?
    a. faulty accommodation
    b. phantom limb pain
    c. perceptual inconstancy
    d. stereochemical abnormalities

31. The gustatory sense refers to the chemical sense of
    a. smell.
    b. taste.
    c. touch.
    d. pain.

32. To how many primary qualities do human taste buds respond?
    a. four
    b. seven
    c. twelve
    d. more than twenty

33. Which of the following is involved in smell?
    a. gustation
    b. olfaction
    c. the vestibular sense
    d. the kinesthetic sense

34. What do all the chemicals that humans can detect as odors have in common?
    a. They all contain an ethereal quality.
    b. They are all organic compounds.
    c. They contain sodium and potassium ions.
    d. They fit like locks into the papillae receptor keys.

35. The Gestalt psychologists described a principle of perception that holds that when we perceive a visual stimulus, part of what we see is the center of attention and the _____; the rest is the _____.
    a. ground; figure
    b. figure; ground
    c. target; figure
    d. target; ground

36. Filling in missing information in our visual perceptions is called
    a. figure-ground.
    b. proximity.
    c. continuity.
    d. similarity.

37. The tendency for perceptions of objects to remain relatively unchanged in spite of changes in raw sensations is called
    a. monocular constancy.
    b. perceptual constancy.
    c. linear perspective.
    d. the figure-ground principle.

38. Artists use many colors to depict a single object because they recognize the influence of light and shadow. This demonstrates an artist's ability to overcome
    a. retinal disparity.
    b. linear perspective.
    c. color constancy.
    d. visual illusion.

39. Retinal disparity is a cue in
    a. color perception.
    b. depth perception.
    c. perceptual organization.
    d. perceptual constancy.

40. Depth perception depends on monocular and binocular cues. Monocular cues are cues
    a. relating to single colors.
    b. relating to single shapes.
    c. available to one eye.
    d. available as the two eyes interact.

41. The fact that what we "see" is not always the same as the visual information that enters our eyes can be demonstrated most dramatically by
    a. perceptual constancies.
    b. visual illusions.
    c. depth perception.
    d. retinal disparity.

42. Line illusions often take advantage of which of the following?
    a. monocular depth cues
    b. retinal disparity
    c. brightness constancy
    d. convergence

43. A research study indicated that sexually aroused males perceive females as being more physically attractive than non-sexually aroused males. This study implicated that which of the following affects perception?
    a. perceptual constancy
    b. learning
    c. motivation
    d. kinesthetics

44. What happens when pygmies who live in the dense rain forests of Africa visit the African plains?
    a. They are fooled by the Zoliner illusion.
    b. They fail to demonstrate size constancy.
    c. They demonstrate a heightened degree of linear perspective.
    d. They are fooled by the superposition illusion.

Chapter 3 Answer Key

1. c	6. a	11. c	16. b	21. d	26. c	31. b	36. c	41. b
2. a	7. b	12. c	17. b	22. c	27. b	32. a	37. b	42. a
3. b	8. c	13. b	18. d	23. b	28. b	33. b	38. c	43. c
4. c	9. c	14. c	19. b	24. c	29. b	34. b	39. b	44. b
5. b	10. c	15. b	20. c	25. b	30. b	35. b	40. c	

4 THE NATURE OF & STATES OF CONSCIOUSNESS

LEARNING OBJECTIVES

1. Define consciousness and compare directed consciousness, flowing consciousness, and daydreams.
2. Explain Hilgard's concept of divided consciousness.
3. Identify the characteristics of the unconscious mind.
4. List and describe the stages of sleep.
5. Compare and contrast REM sleep and non-REM sleep features.
6. Describe what is understood about the content and meaning of dreams.
7. Describe the theories that seek to explain why we sleep and dream.
8. Describe the following sleep phenomena: nightmares, night terrors, sleepwalking, and sleeptalking.
9. Distinguish among the sleep disorders insomnia, narcolepsy, and sleep apnea.
10. Explain circadian and other rhythms and describe the consequences of interrupting circadian rhythms.
11. List the characteristics of altered states of consciousness.
12. Describe the meditation process and the controversy regarding the benefits of meditation.
13. Identify the characteristics of the hypnotic state and describe the relationship between mesmerism and hypnosis.
14. Describe depersonalization and astral projection.
15. Describe the reports of individuals who have had near death experiences.
16. List the variables that influence individual responses to drugs.
17. Distinguish between the risks associated with drug use.
18. Name the four major categories of psychotropic drugs.
19. Explain the effects of stimulants and compare the effects of amphetamines and cocaine.
20. Identify depressant drugs and compare their various effects.
21. Describe the effects of inhalants, hallucinogens, and marijuana.
22. Differentiate between act-alike and designer drugs and explain the dangers of polydrug abuse.

SAMPLE QUESTIONS

1. When a person is aware of events taking place in her or his internal as well as external environment, that person is considered to be in a state of
   a. consciousness.
   b. transcendence.
   c. divided perception.
   d. heightened sensation.

2. When our consciousness is ordered, focused, and one-tracked, such as when we are reading a book, we are probably experiencing _____ consciousness.
   a. flowing
   b. hypnagogic
   c. latent
   d. directed

3. You have just read your psychology assignment for the third time in the last hour. You know you looked at each word and turned all the pages. However, you cannot remember a single word you've read because you keep thinking about your job interview tomorrow. What have you just experienced?
   a. directed consciousness
   b. flowing consciousness
   c. transcendental consciousness
   d. divided consciousness

4. Lindsay has just won the lottery. As she drives to a friend's house to tell her the good news, she is oblivious to the traffic and the route she takes. This probably occurs because of
   a. directed consciousness.
   b. flowing consciousness.
   c. divided consciousness.
   d. depersonalization.

5. Mental processes that occur without a person being aware of them are
   a. daydreams.
   b. unconscious.
   c. hypnagogic.
   d. conscious.

6. When research participants were asked to repeat a message coming in one ear and ignore a message coming in the other ear, what were the researcher's attempting to demonstrate scientifically?
   a. unconscious processing
   b. flowing consciousness
   c. depersonalization
   d. divided consciousness

7. What happens during the hypnagogic state?
   a. deep sleep passes to REM sleep
   b. the number of REM sleep patterns increases
   c. we pass from wakefulness to sleep
   d. we are more susceptible to suggestion

8. A concerned friend told you that as her spouse falls off to sleep his body is prone to sudden jerks. What should you tell her?
    a. Her spouse is a victim of sleep apnea.
    b. Her spouse is experiencing abnormal hypnogogia.
    c. Her spouse may have narcolepsy.
    d. Her spouse is experiencing normal myoclonia.

9. It is 2:00 a.m. and Allison has been sleeping for several hours. Her heart begins to pound and flutter, her fingers twitch, her eyelids flicker, and her breathing becomes shallow and irregular. Sleep researcher Wilse Webb would describe these phenomena as an example of
    a. a night terror.
    b. an autonomic storm.
    c. non-REM dream patterns.
    d. stage one sleep.

10. The difference between REM and non-REM dreams is that
    a. non-REM dreams have more imagery.
    b. REM dreams are less frequent.
    c. non-REM dreams have bizarre content.
    d. non-REM dreams are closer to normal thinking.

11. What did Freud consider to be the "royal road to the unconscious"?
    a. dreams
    b. meditation
    c. the ego
    d. hypnosis

12. What percentage of dreams are completely fantastic and bizarre?
    a. 85
    b. 63
    c. 37
    d. 10

13. The term "sleep debt" describes a condition in which
    a. the sleeper goes immediately into REM sleep.
    b. insomnia develops at night and narcolepsy occurs during the day.
    c. daily naps help a person avoid normal sleeping patterns.
    d. a person is more likely to fall asleep more quickly and sleep longer.

14. What are the most common side effects of minor sleep loss?
    a. irritability, fatigue, and inefficiency
    b. narcolepsy and dreams with latent content
    c. hallucinations and delusions
    d. insomnia, inattention, and increased myoclonia

15. A terrifying kind of dream that occurs during REM sleep and whose content is exceptionally frightening or uncomfortable is referred to as a(n)
    a. nightmare.
    b. night terror.
    c. autonomic storm.
    d. REM fright.

16. A sleep research participant awakened during non-REM sleep screaming, heart pounding, and sweating heavily. What else may the participant report to the sleep researcher?
    a. a vividly frightening dream
    b. a sensation of falling
    c. a strong urge to go back to sleep
    d. no clear recollection of a dream

17. Jerry is in the process of getting a divorce and is having trouble at his job. Previously he has not had any sleep disorders. Which disorder would he most likely develop?
    a. sleep apnea
    b. narcolepsy
    c. insomnia
    d. sleeptalking

18. If you find that you are waking up frequently during the night or often wake up an hour or two before your alarm goes off, you may have
    a. manifest insomnia.
    b. sleep-onset insomnia.
    c. sleep-latency insomnia.
    d. early-awakening insomnia.

19. A class project required a student nurse to make hourly records of her own blood pressure and body temperature over a thirty-day period. When the data were graphed, it became clear that these readings changed in a predictable way on a daily basis. The reason for this regularity is that many physiological processes are
    a. determined by subconscious expectations.
    b. governed by circadian rhythms.
    c. controlled by daily lunar cycles.
    d. correlated with daily lunar cycles.

20. Our body's twenty-four-hour cycles are based on
    a. cultural norms.
    b. the planet's gravity.
    c. lunar cycles.
    d. the earth's daily rotation.

21. What do drugs, trauma, fatigue, hypnosis, and sensory deprivation have in common?
    a. They produce the same brain wave activity.
    b. They produce extreme negative emotional states.
    c. They produce high levels of consciousness
    d. They produce altered states of consciousness

22. Which of the following is a characteristic of altered consciousness?
    a. clear perception
    b. logical thought
    c. a sense of detachment
    d. intense positive emotions

23. An altered state of consciousness, sometimes achieved during meditation, that transcends normal human experience is called
    a. a transcendental mantra.
    b. a transcendental state.
    c. supreme meditation.
    d. astral meditation.

24. Those who wish to reach a more "perfect" state of consciousness other than normal waking consciousness often engage in
    a. hypnotic control.
    b. divided consciousness.
    c. depersonalization.
    d. meditation.

25. In terms of states of consciousness, hypnosis involves a
    a. high degree of controlled processes.
    b. strong defense against suggestibility.
    c. sense of deep relaxation and altered body awareness.
    d. dependence on a belief in supernatural powers.

26. What do most experts believe about hypnotic age regression?
    a. It is very useful in child abuse cases.
    b. It can help people clearly recall painful experiences from the past.
    c. It does not improve the recall of childhood events.
    d. It is only useful for recalling the details of non-traumatic experiences.

27. Depersonalization involves
    a. seeing things that are not seen by others.
    b. hearing voices telling you to do certain things.
    c. feeling unimportant or helpless.
    d. having a sense of being unreal.

28. The perception that your mind has left your body is an example of a general phenomenon known as
    a. mesmerism.
    b. astral meditation.
    c. transcendental state.
    d. astral projection.

29. What do people who have reported near death experiences have in common?
    a. They were not clinically dead.
    b. They still had brain function.
    c. They could not have been affected by drugs.
    d. They were not afraid of death before the experience.

30. Many near death experiences seem to include reports of
    a. hypnagogic states.
    b. mesmerism.
    c. age regression.
    d. astral projection.

31. Gillian bought some cocaine that she felt gave her a great experience. When she bought more cocaine from the same dealer it did not give her the same experience. Given this information, what BEST explains why her experiences differed?

    a. expectation
    b. drug purity
    c. personal characteristics
    d. social situation

32. Personal expectations, social situations, and mood are factors that may
    a. explain why we sleep and dream.
    b. affect the onset of a narcoleptic attack.
    c. influence an individual's response to drugs.
    d. increase the likelihood of astral projection.

33. Whenever John is down or "stressed out," he turns to marijuana. In fact, his friends think John has developed quite a habit, because he has been "relaxing" more and more. It is likely that John is _____ marijuana.
    a. showing tolerance to
    b. showing cross-tolerance to
    c. physiologically addicted to
    d. psychologically dependent on

34. If a person discovers that larger and larger doses of a drug are required to produce the same effect on consciousness, it is likely that he or she has established a
    a. physiological addiction.
    b. psychological dependence.
    c. psychotropic addiction.
    d. psychotropic dependence.

35. Psychotropic drugs are characterized primarily for their ability to
    a. be addictive.
    b. increase sympathetic arousal.
    c. alter conscious experience.
    d. dull awareness.

36. The category of psychotropic drugs that produce dreamlike alterations of perception are called
    a. stimulants.
    b. sedatives.
    c. hypnotics.
    d. hallucinogens.

37. What do Benzedrine, caffeine, and cocaine have in common?
    a. They are in the same category as alcohol and Demerol.
    b. They are all narcotics.
    c. They are all hallucinogens.
    d. They are in the same category as amphetamines.

38. If you took a drug that lessened your feelings of fatigue, created an elevated mood, and decreased your appetite, which of the following did you probably take?
    a. amphetamine
    b. alcohol
    c. heroin
    d. valium

39. Stimulant is to depressant as
    a. alcohol is to cocaine.
    b. codeine is to alcohol.
    c. Dexedrine is to alcohol.
    d. cocaine is to Dexedrine.

40. Tranquilizers and alcohol belong to a drug category called
    a. stimulants.
    b. narcotics.
    c. depressants.
    d. sedatives.

41.   Your neighbor has just confided in you that he is an addict. You have never seen him drink alcohol or pop pills but you have seen many small paper bags lying around his garage. Given this evidence, to which category of drug might your neighbor be addicted?
      a.   hallucinogens
      b.   depressants
      c.   inhalants
      d.   stimulants

42.   Which drug is not physically addictive and after repeated use may take less of the drug to produce the desired effect?
      a.   opium
      b.   marijuana
      c.   LSD
      d.   caffeine

43.   An act-alike drug is composed of _____ substances.
      a.   heroin-like
      b.   amphetamine-like
      c.   legal
      d.   illegal

44.   The use of more than one drug by the same person
      a.   is called designer drug abuse.
      b.   often reflects a history of emotional problems.
      c.   may actually prevent addiction to either drug.
      d.   usually diminishes the effect of each drug.

Chapter 4 Answer Key

1. a	6. a	11. a	16. d	21. d	26. c	31. b	36. d	41. c
2. d	7. c	12. d	17. c	22. d	27. d	32. c	37. d	42. b
3. d	8. d	13. d	18. d	23. b	28. d	33. d	38. a	43. c
4. c	9. b	14. a	19. b	24. d	29. b	34. b	39. c	44. b
5. b	10. d	15. a	20. d	25. c	30. d	35. c	40. c	

5 BASIC PRINCIPLES OF LEARNING

LEARNING OBJECTIVES

1. Identify the key features of the definition of learning.
2. Identify the significant elements in Pavlov's study of classical conditioning; for example, association.
3. Define classical conditioning and its terminology, including UCS, UCR, CS, and CR.
4. Identify applications of classical conditioning and their importance.
5. Identify and define the processes involved in operant conditioning as well as its connection to the "law of effect."
6. Understand how positive reinforcement is influenced by timing, consistency, and individual preferences.
7. Distinguish between primary reinforcement and secondary reinforcement.
8. Compare and contrast the four schedules of reinforcement: fixed ratio, variable ratio, fixed interval, and variable interval.
9. Understand the process of shaping.
10. Define negative reinforcement, and compare escape conditioning to avoidance conditioning.
11. List the dangers of using punishment and identify guidelines for the appropriate use of punishment.
12. Understand the differences between classical and operant conditioning.
13. Distinguish between stimulus discrimination and stimulus generalization.
14. Identify how extinction occurs.
15. Understand how spontaneous recovery and disinhibition are related to extinction.
16. Compare the cognitive and connectionist interpretations of learning.
17. Know the characteristics of place learning, latent learning, insight learning, and learning sets.
18. Define modeling and explain the roles of vicarious reinforcement and vicarious punishment in learning.
19. Know how biological factors affect learning, including learned taste aversions.

SAMPLE QUESTIONS

1. "Any relatively permanent change in behavior" defines
   a. experience.
   b. memory.
   c. learning.
   d. response.

2. An essential factor in the definition of learning is that the learned behavior
   a. must result from maturation.
   b. must be unmotivated.
   c. has a biological cause.
   d. is relatively permanent.

3. In classical conditioning, responses are said to be _____ an organism by a(n) _____.
   a. elicited from; stimulus
   b. initiated by; operant
   c. emitted by; stimulus
   d. operated by; operant

4. In Pavlov's experiments, which condition of association produced the BEST results?
   a. When the metronome preceded the food powder by 10 seconds.
   b. When the food powder and metronome were presented simultaneously.
   c. When the food powder preceded the metronome by 10 seconds.
   d. When the metronome preceded the food powder by 1/2 second.

5. Classical conditioning involves learning
   a. associations between behaviors and consequences.
   b. through the mental manipulation of information.
   c. associations between stimuli.
   d. behaviors through observing others.

6. A fleck of dust or dirt in your eye automatically causes the eye to produce tears to wash the dirt out. What would the fleck of dust or dirt be labeled if it were part of a classical conditioning experiment?
   a. unconditioned stimulus
   b. unconditioned response
   c. conditioned stimulus
   d. conditioned response

7. Joe has been afraid of cats since childhood when he was attacked and scratched by a neighborhood stray. A fear such as Joe's may BEST be explained by
   a. classical conditioning.
   b. observational learning.
   c. operant conditioning.
   d. insight learning.

8. When counterconditioning is used, a conditioned stimulus is paired with an unconditioned stimulus which is _____ the conditioned response.
   a. reinforced by
   b. extinguished by
   c. associated with
   d. incompatible with

9. Which of the following is a key element in operant conditioning?
   a. the type of stimulus used
   b. the nature of the learning task
   c. the consequences of a behavior
   d. whether a response is elicited or not

10. When voluntary behaviors are either strengthened or weakened by their outcomes, the behavioral changes result from
    a. insight learning.
    b. classical conditioning.
    c. observational learning.
    d. operant conditioning.

11. The Smith's new puppy cries in the middle of the night. Various family members periodically check the dog, who responds by happily wagging his tail. Lately, his crying has actually increased. This increase is likely due to
    a. positive punishment.
    b. positive reinforcement.
    c. negative reinforcement.
    d. classical conditioning.

12. A child cries until his mother gives him a piece of candy. The candy is a(n)
    a. conditioned stimulus.
    b. unconditioned response.
    c. positive reinforcer.
    d. secondary reinforcer.

13. Which of the following BEST describes a primary reinforcer?
    a. They are learned in childhood.
    b. They are classically conditioned responses.
    c. They are the same as unconditioned responses.
    d. They are not acquired through learning.

14. Primary reinforcer is to secondary reinforcer as
    a. classical conditioning is to operant conditioning.
    b. operant conditioning is to classical conditioning.
    c. unlearned is to learned.
    d. learned is to unlearned.

15. Assume that your class is going to have an oral quiz on the material in this chapter. For every two questions in a row that a student gets correct, the professor will add one point to the classroom participation grade. This is an example of a _____ schedule of reinforcement.
    a. variable ratio
    b. fixed ratio
    c. fixed interval
    d. variable interval

16. If you give your dog a dog biscuit every fifth time he plays dead, what reinforcement schedule is the dog on?
    a. fixed ratio
    b. fixed interval
    c. variable ratio
    d. variable interval

17. A child is reinforced first for manipulating books, then for looking through them, next for reading them briefly, and last for reading them for longer periods. This procedure is an example of
   a. modeling.
   b. shaping.
   c. classical conditioning.
   d. insight learning.

18. When an instructor commends students for asking tentative questions in order to encourage the asking of more detailed and technical questions, the instructor is using
   a. classical conditioning.
   b. a conditioned response.
   c. shaping.
   d. primary reinforcement.

19. The type of operant conditioning in which a behavior is reinforced because it causes something to end or not to occur is called
   a. negative reinforcement.
   b. negative conditioning.
   c. punishment.
   d. primary punishment.

20. A student comes to college and is extremely anxious about doing poorly and flunking out. The student studies hard and receives all A's the first semester. This student has been
   a. positively reinforced.
   b. negatively reinforced.
   c. classically conditioned.
   d. vicariously punished.

21. "Increase behavior" is to "decrease behavior" as
   a. positive reinforcement is to negative reinforcement.
   b. punishment is to positive reinforcement.
   c. negative reinforcement is to punishment.
   d. punishment is to primary reinforcement.

22. Mr. Harper used to yell at Mrs. Harper for trumping cards unnecessarily when they played bridge. Instead of improving her play, Mrs. Harper gave up bridge altogether. This is an example of which danger associated with punishment?
   a. The punished individual can turn the punishment into reinforcement.
   b. The punished individual can learn to dislike the punisher.
   c. Punishment can have a generalized inhibiting effect.
   d. The punisher feels reinforced for giving out punishment.

23. Classical conditioning and operant conditioning differ from each other in that operant conditioning
   a. involves reflexive or involuntary behavior.
   b. occurs independently of behavior.
   c. occurs only if the response being conditioned has been emitted.
   d. is not contingent on the occurrence of a response.

24. Which of the following behaviors would most likely be involved in classical conditioning?
   a. lever pressing
   b. eye blinking
   c. maze running
   d. hand raising

25. John loves to receive mail. Over the years, he has learned to tell the difference between the sound of the mail truck and the other cars and trucks that pass his house. What process is at work here?
    a. stimulus discrimination
    b. stimulus generalization
    c. response generalization
    d. vicarious reinforcement

26. A pigeon learned to peck a lighted disc for a few bits of grain. The bird does not peck when the light is off because no grain will be forthcoming. The light is called the
    a. generalized stimulus.
    b. conditioned stimulus.
    c. conditioned response.
    d. discriminative stimulus.

27. How does extinction occur in classical conditioning?
    a. When the CS is presented without the UCS.
    b. When the CR is presented without the UCR
    c. When the emitted response is negatively reinforced.
    d. When the emitted response is punished.

28. You trained a rat to press a lever using positive reinforcement. When the behavior was well learned you stopped giving the reward for the lever-pressing behavior. Most likely you discovered that the
    a. lever pressing behavior increased.
    b. rat developed an avoidance response.
    c. lever-pressing behavior was extinguished.
    d. rat learned stimulus discrimination.

29. When a conditioned response that was extinguished suddenly returns after an interval of rest, what has occurred?
    a. external disinhibition
    b. internal disinhibition
    c. negative reinforcement
    d. spontaneous recovery

30. When a rest period is allowed to occur following the extinction of a CR there is often a recurrence of the CR when the subject is returned to the experimental situation and presented with the CS. This is called
    a. spontaneous recovery.
    b. discriminative remission.
    c. superstitious behavior.
    d. stimulus generalization.

31. The cognitive and connectionist views of learning
    a. are very similar theoretically.
    b. explain how neural associations are formed.
    c. are opposing theories about what happens during learning.
    d. were both developed and tested by Albert Bandura.

32. Which of the following pioneers in the field of learning would most likely support the connectionist theory of learning?
    a. Edward Tolman
    b. Wolfgang Kohler
    c. Albert Bandura
    d. B.F. Skinner

33. Which of the following is <u>BEST</u> associated with place learning?
    a. acquiring fixed patterns of muscle movements result in a correct solution
    b. acquiring knowledge of the location of the reinforcer
    c. learning based on some instinctive, unlearned capacity
    d. kinesthetic and proprioceptive feedback are primary cues in problem solving

34. Edward Tolman developed some ingenious experiments that involved timing how fast rats could run through mazes to reach a reward. The experiments tended to support
    a. the cognitive view of learning.
    b. classical conditioning.
    c. the connectionist view of learning.
    d. vicarious reinforcement.

35. A basic assumption underlying modeling is that
    a. some learning may occur without reinforcement.
    b. observational learning is not true learning.
    c. all learning occurs by imitation.
    d. all reinforcement occurs vicariously.

36. Learning acquired through observation is referred to as
    a. modeling.
    b. acquired learning.
    c. operant learning.
    d. insight learning.

37. The fact that it is easier to condition a fear of things that have some intrinsic association with danger suggests that people are _____ prepared to learn certain kinds of fear.
    a. psychologically
    b. biologically
    c. intuitively
    d. latently

38. What best explains the fact that human phobias are most often developed in response to intrinsically dangerous stimuli?
    a. classical conditioning
    b. biological preparedness
    c. operant conditioning
    d. insight learning

Chapter 5 Answer Key

1. c	6. a	11. b	16. a	21. c	26. d	31. c	36. a
2. d	7. a	12. c	17. b	22. c	27. a	32. d	37. b
3. a	8. d	13. d	18. c	23. c	28. c	33. b	38. b
4. d	9. c	14. c	19. a	24. b	29. d	34. a	
5. c	10. d	15. b	20. b	25. a	30. a	35. a	

6 MEMORY, LEARNING, & BEHAVIOR

LEARNING OBJECTIVES

1. Identify the operations involved in the information-processing view of memory and understand the stage theory of memory.
2. Know the characteristics of the sensory register.
3. Define short-term memory and understand how its life span and capacity can be influenced.
4. Distinguish how long-term memory differs from short-term memory.
5. Describe the three kinds of long-term memory: procedural, episodic, and semantic.
6. Understand how information is organized in long-term memory.
7. Identify different ways of measuring the retrieval of information from long-term memory and explain serial learning and the "tip of the tongue phenomenon."
8. Distinguish between deep and shallow processing in the levels of processing model and understand the role of elaboration.
9. Distinguish among the four major theories of forgetting and recognize the terms or processes associated with decay theory, interference theory, reconstruction theory, and motivated forgetting.
10. Recognize and understand synaptic theories of memory.
11. Distinguish between anterograde amnesia and retrograde amnesia.
12. Recognize how drugs may or may not enhance memory.

SAMPLE QUESTIONS

1. Which of the following are the operations associated with the information-processing model of memory?
    a. input, storage, and retrieval
    b. encode, rehearse, and process
    c. process, rehearse, and recall
    d. input, rehearsal, and output

2. Sensory information must be _____ before it can be _____.
    a. rehearsed; encoded
    b. searched; consolidated
    c. encoded; controlled
    d. encoded; stored

3. Which of the following is the most temporary stage of memory?
    a. short-term memory
    b. episodic memory
    c. the sensory register
    d. semantic memory

4. You are reading a book and your friend John asks you a question. By the time you say, "What did you say?" you "hear" his question. This is due to storage of information in _____ for audition.
    a. short-term memory
    b. long-term memory
    c. working memory
    d. the sensory register

5. The memory stage where information is stored temporarily is referred to as the _____ stage.
    a. selecting
    b. long-term memory
    c. sensory-processing
    d. short-term memory

6. Rehearsal and chunking are _____ processes that are applied during _____ memory.
    a. encoding; long-term
    b. retrieval; long-term
    c. control; short-term
    d. procedural; short-term

7. Long-term memory is to short-term memory as
    a. exhaustive is to indexed.
    b. acoustic code is to semantic code.
    c. rehearsal is to chunking.
    d. permanent is to temporary.

8. Unlike forgetting in short-term memory, forgetting in long-term memory is due to
    a. memory decay.
    b. elaborative transfer.
    c. retrieval problems.
    d. the passage of time.

9. Sometimes people cannot remember a phone number until they move their fingers as if they were dialing. This is an example of
    a. procedural memory.
    b. declarative memory.
    c. effortful encoding.
    d. proactive disinhibition.

10. Mary, whose hobby is the study of whales, tells her teacher all about the buluga whale, even though she has never actually seen one. Mary's information is stored as _____ memory.
    a. cued
    b. motivated
    c. episodic
    d. semantic

11. The organization of information in LTM is important for
    a. increasing capacity.
    b. facilitating retrieval.
    c. understanding chunking.
    d. temporary storage.

12. In a research study, participants were shown real words and made-up words and asked to respond to them by pressing a yes or no button. The researchers were interested in the reaction times for the responses to real words. According to the results of the study, the reaction time for the word <u>cow</u> would be increased if a(n) _____ word preceded its presentation.
    a. made-up
    b. elaborative
    c. look alike
    d. related

13. Essay examination is to multiple-choice test as
    a. recognition is to relearning.
    b. recall is to relearning.
    c. recognition is to recall.
    d. recall is to recognition.

14. Which of the following is the most sensitive method of evaluating memory?
    a. recall
    b. recognition
    c. rehearsal
    d. relearning

15. A model of memory that provides an alternative to the traditional three-stage model is the _____ model.
    a. synaptic facilitation
    b. declarative/procedural
    c. levels of processing
    d. serial learning

16. According to Craik and Lockhart's levels of processing model, STM and LTM are
    a. part of the same memory store.
    b. separate stages of memory.
    c. only two stages of a five-stage theory.
    d. forms of declarative memory.

17. What causes forgetting to occur according to the decay theory?
    a. unpleasant experiences
    b. the passage of time
    c. unconscious motivations
    d. interference by new material

18. The theory of forgetting that states that the memory trace actually fades over time is the _____ theory.
    a. motivated forgetting
    b. decay
    c. reconstruction
    d. interference

19. Another name for "memory trace" is
    a. engram.
    b. chunk.
    c. synapse.
    d. potentiation.

20. Simple forms of learning, such as classically conditioning the gill withdrawal reflex in the sea snail, appear to physically take place
    a. when electric shock is present.
    b. only in creatures without a brain.
    c. at the synaptic level.
    d. outside of the nervous system.

21. A memory disorder in which one cannot store or retrieve new information in the long-term memory is called
    a. anterograde amnesia.
    b. retrograde amnesia.
    c. Korsakoff's psychosis.
    d. Alzheimer's.

22. Suppose a person is injected with a drug that leaves current memory intact, but the drug prevents new information from passing from short-term to long-term memory. This drug would produce
    a. anterograde amnesia.
    b. retrograde amnesia.
    c. relearning interference.
    d. proactive amnesia.

23. The formation of memory is disrupted by drugs that block the action of
    a. epinephrine.
    b. dopamine.
    c. endorphin.
    d. acetylcholine.

24. In a research study, under which condition did college students' have more accurate memories?
    a. when their blood sugar was high
    b. when they were under hypnosis
    c. when asked leading questions
    d. when acetylcholine blockers were administered

Chapter 6 Answer Key

1. a	6. c	11. b	16. a	21. a
2. d	7. d	12. d	17. b	22. a
3. c	8. c	13. d	18. b	23. d
4. d	9. a	14. d	19. a	24. a
5. d	10. d	15. c	20. c	

7 COGNITION, LANGUAGE, & INTELLIGENCE

LEARNING OBJECTIVES

1. Define cognition and know its three primary facets.
2. Understand what concepts are and distinguish between simple and complex concepts.
3. Recognize the processes involved in concept formation.
4. Distinguish between the basic and prototypical characteristics of natural concepts.
5. Define problem solving and recognize the three major types of cognitive operations involved in problem solving.
6. Distinguish among the following problem-solving strategies: trial-and-error, algorithmic, and heuristic.
7. Define artificial intelligence and recognize how it is used in problem-solving.
8. Identify the major characteristics of human experts.
9. Define creativity and distinguish between convergent thinking and divergent thinking.
10. List the four steps involved in Wallas's description of creative problem solving.
11. Recognize three ways that enhance creative thinking and list the ways in which Sternberg thinks creative thinkers different from other people.
12. Define language, including the meaning of semantic content, the distinction between the surface structure of language and the deep structure of language, and the generative property of language.
13. Distinguish among phonemes, morphemes, and syntax.
14. Understand the Whorfian hypothesis and recognize its significance.
15. Know the research results regarding the language capabilities of animals.
16. Define intelligence and compare the position of psychologists who view intelligence as a general ability to those who view it as several specific abilities.
17. List Sternberg's cognitive components of intelligence and distinguish between the components of his triarchic theory of intelligence.
18. Distinguish between fluid intelligence and crystallized intelligence.
19. Recognize the importance of intelligence in modern society.
20. Identify intelligence tests and how they are useful.
21. Understand the concept of intelligence quotient and distinguish between ratio IQ and deviation IQ.
22. List the characteristics of good intelligence tests.
23. Recognize the predictive abilities of intelligence tests and understand the concept of everyday intelligence.
24. Identify the factors that contribute to an individual's intelligence.
25. Identify the ethnic differences in intelligence scores and know the issues related to these differences.
26. Distinguish between mental retardation and giftedness.

SAMPLE QUESTIONS

1. Considering perception, memory, thinking, and language, which is an intellectual process?
   a. Thinking is the only intellectual process.
   b. Only memory and thinking are intellectual processes.
   c. Only thinking and language are intellectual processes.
   d. All are intellectual processes.

2. Complete the following statement with one of the primary facets of cognition. Cognition
   a. is the basic unit of thinking.
   b. is a mental set.
   c. processes information.
   d. senses internal stimuli.

3. A category for organizing objects and events in the environment is called a
   a. theory.
   b. hypothesis.
   c. principle.
   d. concept.

4. "All objects that are both furry and brown," is an example of a _____ concept.
   a. disjunctive
   b. conjunctive
   c. conditional
   d. natural

5. As a research participant you were shown cards imprinted with combinations of numbers, symbols, and colors. As the cards were shown to you one-at-a-time, the experimenter gave you feedback about your answer as to whether a card belonged in a certain group or not. What was the experimenter likely studying?
   a. perceptual processes
   b. the Whorfian hypothesis
   c. concept formation
   d. fluid intelligence

6. If you test hypotheses about the defining characteristics of a category, you are <u>MOST</u> <u>LIKELY</u> engaging in
   a. formal experimentation.
   b. concept formation.
   c. artificial intelligence.
   d. problem solving.

7. Concepts that are learned more easily than others are called _____ concepts.
   a. simple
   b. subordinate
   c. conjunctive
   d. natural

8. According to Eleanor Rosch, which of the following concepts would be easiest for a human to learn?
   a. dogs
   b. beagles
   c. animals
   d. guard dogs

9. When information is used to reach a goal that is blocked, what is the cognitive process called?
    a. concept formation
    b. conjunctive thinking
    c. problem solving
    d. neural pruning

10. We tend to use certain steps in the solution of a problem. Before we can understand the elements of a problem, we must _____ the problem.
    a. formulate
    b. generate
    c. analyze
    d. evaluate

11. You make your famous strawberry banana daiquiris for a gathering of your best friends. You use a recipe to ensure the correct combination of ingredients. Which approach to problem solving was used in this example?
    a. trial-and-error
    b. heuristics
    c. expert systems
    d. algorithm

12. In solving problems, rather than testing all possible solutions, people rely on principles that allow them to test solutions more selectively. These principles are known as
    a. algorithms.
    b. heuristics.
    c. prototypes.
    d. morphemes.

13. Artificial intelligence is used as a model by psychologists to study
    a. learning processes.
    b. computer science.
    c. human cognition.
    d. concept formation.

14. In the area of artificial intelligence, what are expert systems?
    a. narrowly focused computer problem solving programs
    b. computer programs that replace physicians
    c. computer programs that solve a wide range of problems
    d. computer programs that model divergent thinking

15. Which of the following is a characteristic of expertise?
    a. limited to specific areas
    b. high degree of risk taking
    c. low level of awareness of errors
    d. focus on one task at a time

16. What advantage do experts have over novices?
    a. Experts have a broad level of basic knowledge.
    b. Experts are not affected by mental sets in all areas of problem solving.
    c. Experts recognize patterns more often and more quickly.
    d. Experts focus on one problem at a time.

17. When asked what a hanger is useful for, a child says it is useful for hanging clothes. This demonstrates
    a. convergent thinking.
    b. disjunctive thinking.
    c. illumination.
    d. an algorithm.

18. A test that requires you to select the best or correct answer to a problem is requiring you to use _____ thinking.
    a. parallel
    b. algorithmic
    c. convergent
    d. serial

19. After working on a calculus problem for three hours, Sue took a two-hour break before going back to the problem. She solved the problem soon after she returned to it. Sue used a technique called _____, which can often be an aid to problem solving.
    a. relaxation
    b. preparation
    c. incubation
    d. meditation

20. In the process of problem solving suggested by Wallas, incubation is followed by
    a. illumination.
    b. preparation.
    c. verification.
    d. acknowledgment.

21. Hayes described three ways of making creative thinking more likely to occur. The first step is to
    a. take a rest from the problem.
    b. suggest possible solutions.
    c. develop a knowledge base.
    d. consider basic analogies.

22. Which of the following is NOT suggested as a way to enhance creative thinking?
    a. build a knowledge base
    b. use prescriptive rules
    c. consider analogies to solved problems
    d. be persistent

23. The meaning of a statement is regarded as its
    a. semantic content.
    b. syntax structure.
    c. surface structure.
    d. phoneme structure.

24. According to Chomsky, the meaning of a statement is found in its
    a. phonemes.
    b. deep structure.
    c. syntax.
    d. surface structure.

25. The basic units of sound in a language are called
    a. morphemes.
    b. syntax.
    c. holophrases.
    d. phonemes.

26. How many phonemes are there in the English language?
    a. 26
    b. 44
    c. approximately 12,000
    d. an infinite number of

27. The notion that the more vocabulary or categories a language has, the more varied our perceptions will be, is a theory connected to
    a. Rosch.
    b. Chomsky.
    c. Miller.
    d. Whorf.

28. People who believe we should substitute gender-neutral terms for masculine terms often believe that _____ influences _____.
    a. language; thought
    b. semantics; syntax
    c. perception; language
    d. thought; intelligence

29. Several efforts have been made to teach apes human language. Although there have been varying degrees of success, the big issue seems to be whether apes
    a. have the anatomy for speech.
    b. have the intelligence for speech.
    c. can generate new combinations of language.
    d. can be taught American Sign Language.

30. Washoe, the chimp raised by the Gardners, was taught to communicate through
    a. spoken language.
    b. facial expressions.
    c. American Sign Language.
    d. Universal Sign Language.

31. The ability of an individual to learn from experience, to reason, and to adapt is a definition of
    a. cognition.
    b. creativity.
    c. language.
    d. intelligence.

32. The person who popularized the term intelligence and believed that intelligence was inherited was
    a. Galton.
    b. Spearman.
    c. Darwin.
    d. Binet.

33. Sternberg's triarchic theory of intelligence is an advance over previous theories of intelligence because it
    a. identifies the steps in intelligent reasoning.
    b. describes the steps in intelligent reasoning.
    c. provides a basis for discovering how some people are more intelligent.
    d. takes into account all aspects of intellectual functioning.

34. According to Sternberg, encoding, inferring, mapping, applying, comparing, and responding are all
    a. aspects of long-term memory.
    b. cognitive steps in intellectual behavior.
    c. components of functional fixedness.
    d. skills used in deep structuring.

35. Which of Sternberg's components of intelligence is MOST similar to fluid intelligence?
    a. knowledge-acquisition components
    b. performance components
    c. the general component
    d. artistic components

36. The ability to learn or invent new strategies for dealing with new problems is called
    a. a mental set.
    b. expertise.
    c. fluid intelligence.
    d. specific intelligence.

37. The text contends that in modern society occupation is overly associated with
    a. pay.
    b. intelligence.
    c. technology.
    d. performance.

38. The average IQ of doctors and lawyers is
    a. 85.
    b. 100.
    c. 112.
    d. 125.

39. Intelligence is a very difficult concept to define. Some psychologists refer to intelligence as
    a. something with which one is born.
    b. something that only develops with experience.
    c. what intelligence tests measure.
    d. how people deal with the real world.

40. What do Terman and Wechsler have in common?
    a. Both studied language in apes.
    b. Both developed intelligence tests.
    c. Both believe intelligence tests are useless.
    d. Both are experts in the field of problem-solving.

41. According to the original Stanford-Binet, IQ was calculated as mental age _____ chronological age, and the result _____ by 100.
    a. divided by; divided
    b. divided by; multiplied
    c. subtracted from; divided
    d. subtracted from; multiplied

42. If a child's mental age were higher than his or her chronological age, this would mean that
    a. the child is brighter than normal.
    b. the child is about average.
    c. the child is less intelligent than normal.
    d. a calculation error was made.

43. A standardized test means that the test can
    a. be used cross-culturally.
    b. measure what it is supposed to measure.
    c. be used in a consistent manner.
    d. be compared to other tests of the same nature.

44. Reading the identical directions to every person taking a given intelligence test is an aspect of the test's
    a. reliability.
    b. validity.
    c. normalization.
    (d.) standardization.

45. Considering three children with IQs of 97, 91, and 106, which one will perform better in school?
    (a.) the one with IQ of 106
    b. the one with IQ of 97
    c. the ones with IQs of 106 and 97
    d. cannot predict confidently

46. How precise are intelligence tests?
    a. very accurate in most cases
    b. not good in extreme cases
    (c.) best at predicting school achievement
    d. best at measuring everyday intelligence

47. Correlations between the intelligence scores of identical twins tend to be
    (a.) high.
    b. low.
    c. the same.
    d. normative.

48. IQs of adopted children are
    (a.) more similar to their biological parents than to their adoptive parents.
    b. more similar to their adoptive parents than to their biological parents.
    c. equally similar to adoptive and biological parents.
    d. uncorrelated to either their adoptive parents or their biological parents.

49. If an intelligence test contains a true cultural bias against a certain group, you would expect the school performance of that group to be
    (a.) better than the test predicts.
    b. worse than the test predicts.
    c. about the same as the test predicts.
    d. unrelated to the test results.

50. Which of the following is true concerning cultural differences in intelligence scores?
    a. Available data support a genetic interpretation.
    b. The gap between white and black scores has widened.
    (c.) Available data support an environmental interpretation.
    d. The differences are intellectually based not cultural.

51. Profoundly retarded is a label given to individuals with IQs under
    a. 50.
    b. 30.
    c. 20.
    d. 10.

52. Along with IQ, giftedness is also associated with
    a. expertise.
    (b.) creativity.
    c. convergent thinking.
    d. crystallized intelligence.

Chapter 7 Answer Key

1. a	6. b	11. d	16. c	21. c	26. b	31. d	36. c	41. b	46. c	51. c
2. c	7. d	12. b	17. a	22. b	27. d	32. a	37. b	42. a	47. a	52. b
3. d	8. a	13. c	18. c	23. a	28. a	33. c	38. d	43. c	48. a	
4. b	9. c	14. a	19. c	24. b	29. c	34. b	39. c	44. d	49. a	
5. c	10. a	15. a	20. a	25. d	30. c	35. a	40. b	45. a	50. c	

8 HUMAN DEVELOPMENT THROUGH THE LIFESPAN

LEARNING OBJECTIVES

1. Understand the interplay of nature and nurture in development and know what role maturation plays in development.
2. Know what imprinting is and recognize the importance of critical periods.
3. From the Harlows' research, recognize the role of early experiences on development.
4. Understand the meaning of individual variation in development.
5. Identify the characteristics common to stage theories of development.
6. Recognize and understand Kohlberg's three levels of moral reasoning: premoral, conventional, and principled.
7. Identify and understand Gilligan's three levels of moral reasoning: individual survival, self-sacrifice, and equality.
8. Compare and contrast Gilligan's and Kohlberg's theories.
9. Recognize the features of Erikson's stage theory of personality development and list the stages of personality development.
10. Differentiate between the developmental stages termed the neonatal period and infancy.
11. Identify the cognitive, emotional, and social aspects of development during the infancy.
12. Identify the cognitive, emotional, and social aspects of development during early childhood.
13. Identify the cognitive, emotional, and social aspects of development during middle childhood.
14. Know what changes occur in physical development during puberty, including primary and secondary sex characteristics, menarche, and the adolescent growth spurt.
15. Identify the characteristics of formal operational thinking and know the characteristics of adolescent egocentrism.
16. Know the research results on adolescent social and emotional development.
17. Identify the physical and cognitive aspects of development in adulthood.
18. Recognize aspects of emotional and social development in adulthood.
19. Contrast Erikson's and Levinson's views of adult personality development.
20. Define climacteric and know how it affects men and women.
21. Know the biological and psychological changes that are involved in aging and recognize the factors associated with "happy aging" and longevity.
22. Identify the controversies associated with stage theories of adulthood.
23. Name and understand the stages of dying identified by Kübler-Ross.

SAMPLE QUESTIONS

1. Developmental psychology is best described as a study of
   a. children from birth through puberty.
   b. children from birth to adulthood.
   c. children, adolescents, and the elderly.
   d. the entire life span, from birth to death.

2. The term <u>maturation</u> refers to systematic changes of the body brought about by
   a. environment.
   b. learning.
   c. physical growth.
   d. nurture.

3. In his studies of imprinting, Konrad Lorenz was giving support to the importance of
   a. maturation.
   b. animism.
   c. social isolation.
   d. early experience.

4. Which of the following illustrates the principle of a critical period?
   a. learning to ride a bicycle when physically mature
   b. developing secondary sexual characteristics
   c. an animal who can only learn to hunt from its mother at a certain age
   d. learning to hop only after learning to walk

5. What did the Harlows demonstrate about social deprivation in monkeys?
   a. It had no long-lasting effects.
   b. It affected the monkey's intelligence.
   c. It slowed down maturation.
   d. It reduced the monkeys' parenting ability.

6. What does research suggest about the permanence of the influence of early abnormal experiences on human development?
   a. Early abnormal experiences produce irreversible damage to social development.
   b. Humans are affected by early abnormal experiences similar to Harlows' monkeys.
   c. Psychologists agree that abnormal early development can be reversed before age 15 years.
   d. Psychologists disagree about the permanence of abnormal early experiences on human development.

7. When comparing many children of the same age, we can say with certainty that development is
   a. constant.
   b. variable.
   c. fixed.
   d. nonexistent.

8. Fred read that children usually learn to walk by age 12 months. If Fred's little boy is not walking at 13½ months, should Fred by concerned?
   a. Yes, the child has passed the critical period for walking.
   b. Yes, the child is maturationally delayed.
   c. Yes, the child's sensorimotor skills are lagging.
   d. No, children develop at different rates.

9. Which of the following do developmental stage theorists tend to support?
   a. a belief that maturation is biologically programmed
   b. a belief in the gradual change model
   c. an indifference to maturation
   d. the nurture aspect of the nature-nurture issue

10. Theorists who believe that children must pass through the same qualitatively different developmental phases in the same order are known as
   a. stage theorists.
   b. continuity theorists.
   c. functionalists.
   d. behaviorists.

11. Which of the following is the correct order of stages in Kohlberg's theory of moral development?
   a. premoral, conventional, principled
   b. preconventional, principled, moral
   c. preoperational, conventional, principled
   d. premoral, principled, conventional

12. Higher levels of moral development reflect an increase in
   a. understanding rules and laws.
   b. concern over the ethics of a person's actions.
   c. the consequences of a person's actions.
   d. doing what society thinks is right.

13. In the first level of Gilligan's theory of moral development, children are concerned with
   a. what is good for him or her.
   b. the approval of others.
   c. whether their parents will love them.
   d. their own sense of right and wrong.

14. Brenda doesn't believe Joan should get a three week paid vacation until everyone at the office can have three week paid vacations. At what level of moral development is Brenda MOST likely operating?
   a. Kohlberg's second level
   b. Gilligan's third level
   c. morality as self-sacrifice
   d. morality as self-serving

15. While Kohlberg's theory reflects a justice perspective, Gilligan's theory reflects a _____ perspective.
   a. concern
   b. communication
   c. value
   d. response

16. What do Kohlberg and Gilligan's first levels of moral development have in common?
   a. children have no sense of morality
   b. rewards are sought and punishment is avoided
   c. self-sacrifice and the approval of others
   d. one's own principles of morality are employed

17. Erikson views early adulthood as a period during which the person is building a network of social relationships and making close contact with potential mates. The crisis experience at this time is
   a. identity vs. identity diffusion.
   b. intimacy vs. isolation.
   c. generativity vs. stagnation.
   d. integrity vs. despair.

18. The first stage of Erikson's stages of personality development is
    a. autonomy vs. shame and doubt.
    b. basic trust vs. mistrust.
    c. autonomy vs. identity.
    d. basic trust vs. autonomy.

19. The neonatal period extends from
    a. 28 weeks gestation to birth.
    b. 38 weeks gestation to birth.
    c. birth to 2 weeks.
    d. birth to 6 weeks.

20. What BEST distinguishes the infancy stage from other stages of development?
    a. physical growth is most rapid in the first year
    b. cognitive growth is 5 times greater than in any other developmental stage
    c. emotions are fully developed before the next developmental stage
    d. it is the only stage that has no emotional development

21. The stage of cognitive development that occurs between birth and age 2 is characterized by mainly reflexive behavior and is termed
    a. the preconventional stage.
    b. the preoperational stage.
    c. concrete operational stage.
    d. None of the other alternatives are correct.

22. What three emotions are neonates capable of expressing?
    a. pleasure, fear, and anger
    b. surprise, pleasure, and distress
    c. shyness, pleasure, and anger
    d. pleasure, anger, and distress

23. Which of Piaget's stages of cognitive development is characterized by egocentric thought?
    a. sensorimotor
    b. preoperational
    c. concrete operational
    d. formal operational

24. A young child looks out the window and sees that it is raining. He assumes that it is raining everywhere, because his thought is characterized by
    a. animism.
    b. egocentrism.
    c. irreversibility.
    d. conservation.

25. Between ages 7 and 11, many of the restrictions of earlier patterns disappear and children can think in sophisticated ways as long as what they are thinking about is tangibly represented. Piaget calls this stage
    a. concrete operations.
    b. formal operations.
    c. preoperational thought.
    d. sensorimotor limits.

26. If a child recognizes that changes in the shape of a clay ball do not change the amount of clay in the ball, the child has demonstrated
    a. object permanence.
    b. formal operations.
    c. reversibility.
    d. conservation.

27. The process of sexual maturation that takes place at the beginning of adolescence is known as
    a. sex typing.
    b. animism.
    c. puberty.
    d. menarche.

28. The more obvious physical changes that occur during puberty are called
    a. primary sex characteristics.
    b. secondary sex characteristics.
    c. climacteric sex characteristics.
    d. tertiary sex characteristics.

29. An adolescent who hypothesizes and speaks in terms of possibilities may well be functioning in the cognitive stage of
    a. formal operational thought.
    b. concrete operational thought.
    c. moral realistic thought.
    d. transductive thought.

30. Bob has an unknown liquid and must determine what it is. He decides to use a number of tests systematically to determine what it is. What stage of cognitive development has Bob reached?
    a. sensorimotor
    b. preoperational
    c. concrete operational
    d. formal operational

31. During which stage of social development do peer relationships become the most important relationship?
    a. early childhood
    b. middle childhood
    c. adolescence
    d. early adulthood

32. If you were to study the basic values of adolescents, such as attitudes toward work, saving money, and competition, you would probably find them to be similar to those
    a. of their parents.
    b. of their peers.
    c. held by their fathers.
    d. held by their teachers.

33. Compared to individuals in their 20s, individuals in their 70s showed declines in
    a. short-term memory.
    b. long-term memory.
    c. transfer from long-term memory.
    d. recalling words without cues.

34. Mr. Anderson is approaching his 70th birthday, and has been healthy all his life. If he is given an intelligence test, it will probably show
    a. a major decline in intelligence because of age.
    b. deficits in memory and vocabulary.
    c. significant deficits in mathematical abilities.
    d. no significant declines.

35. One trait that seems to be stable over the course of adulthood is
    a. desire for power.
    b. comfort.
    c. aggressiveness.
    d. self-consciousness.

36. Which of the following traits tends to decline through adulthood?
    a. enjoyment of being with others
    b. desire for power
    c. enjoyment of excitement
    d. insightfulness

37. Erikson's early adulthood challenge involves
    a. generativity vs. stagnation.
    b. integrity vs. despair.
    c. intimacy vs. isolation.
    d. midlife crisis.

38. According to Levinson, the stage of adult development that occurs anytime from the late twenties to the early thirties is called
    a. the age thirty transition.
    b. culmination.
    c. settling down.
    d. early adulthood.

39. What is the average age of menopause?
    a. 10 to 12 years
    b. 34 to 38 years
    c. 46 to 48 years
    d. 52 to 54 years

40. Women can no longer reproduce when they reach the period known as
    a. menarche.
    b. midlife transition.
    c. the climacteric.
    d. transitional generativity.

41. The older adult who sees meaning in his or her life continues to live a satisfying existence. Erikson refers to this as
    a. despair.
    b. generativity.
    c. intimacy.
    d. integrity.

42. Which of the following is a key psychological variable of happy aging?
    a. lowering activity levels
    b. involuntary retirement
    c. cessation of drinking and smoking
    d. ignoring myths about old age

43. One problem with stage theories is that they suggest
    a. variability of development.
    b. we all develop at the same rate.
    c. universal, unidirectional stages.
    d. individual maturation over time.

44. Studies have indicated that the "midlife crisis" is
    a. very common during the early 40s.
    b. associated with emotional instability.
    c. more common in women than men.
    d. associated with loss of a spouse.

45. Kübler-Ross identified the stages experienced by terminally ill patients and placed them in the order of
    a. anger, denial, depression, bargaining, acceptance.
    b. acceptance, bargaining, anger, denial, depression.
    c. denial, anger, bargaining, depression, acceptance.
    d. denial, bargaining, anger, depression, acceptance.

46. According to Kübler-Ross, what is the first stage of dying?
    a. denial
    b. bargaining
    c. anger
    d. depression

Chapter 8 Answer Key

1. d	6. d	11. a	16. b	21. d	26. d	31. c	36. b	41. d	46. a
2. c	7. b	12. b	17. b	22. b	27. c	32. b	37. c	42. d	
3. d	8. d	13. a	18. b	23. b	28. b	33. d	38. a	43. c	
4. c	9. a	14. b	19. c	24. b	29. a	34. d	39. c	44. b	
5. d	10. a	15. a	20. a	25. a	30. d	35. d	40. c	45. c	

9 MOTIVATION & EMOTION

LEARNING OBJECTIVES

1. Distinguish between motivation and emotion.
2. Recognize the relationship between primary motives and homeostatic mechanisms.
3. Understand the biological and psychological regulation of hunger.
4. Understand the biological and psychological regulation of thirst.
5. Define psychological motive and recognize the following psychological motives: the need for novel stimulation, the need for affiliation, and the need for achievement.
6. Distinguish between optimal arousal theory and the Yerkes-Dodson law.
7. Compare research findings regarding the fear of failure and the fear of success.
8. Understand Solomon's opponent-process theory of motivation.
9. Distinguish between intrinsic and extrinsic motivation.
10. Identify the components of Maslow's hierarchy of motives.
11. Recognize elements associated with definitions of emotion.
12. Distinguish among the James-Lange theory, the Cannon-Bard theory, and the cognitive theory of emotion.
13. Identify the elements associated with lie detection and understand lie detection's effectiveness.
14. Recognize the role of learning and culture in emotions.
15. Distinguish among the following theories of aggression: Freud's instinct theory, the frustration-aggression theory, and the social learning theory.
16. Recognize associations between culture and aggressive behavior and between violent youth gangs and their environment.

SAMPLE QUESTIONS

1. Because motivation cannot be directly observed, it must be inferred from
   a. psychophysiology.
   b. emotions.
   c. behaviors.
   d. EEG patterns.

2. Motivation is studied by psychologists concerned with forces that move an organism to
   a. think.
   b. act.
   c. feel.
   d. die.

3. Most often, motives that involve extremes of comfort or are actually involved in survival are called _____ motives.
   a. secondary
   b. hierarchical
   c. primary
   d. basic

4. Of the following primary motives, which is the best understood?
   a. sleep
   b. hunger
   c. sex
   d. warmth

5. A brain area important in the regulation of hunger and satiety is the
   a. hippocampus.
   b. cerebrum.
   c. hypothalamus.
   d. midbrain.

6. If the feeding center in a rat's hypothalamus is destroyed, what will happen to the rat's behavior?
   a. The rat will continue to eat normally.
   b. The rat will crave fat laden foods.
   c. The rat will stop eating.
   d. The rat will over eat to obesity.

7. Even though the center for hunger and thirst is in the _____, different _____ are involved.
   a. liver; incentives
   b. kidneys; insulin levels
   c. small intestine; receptor sites
   d. hypothalamus; neurotransmitters

8. Surgical destruction of the drink center causes an animal to
   a. have a very dry mouth.
   b. drink excessive amounts of water.
   c. refuse water.
   d. secrete ADH.

9. Experience tends to have a more variable influence on
   a. psychological motives.
   b. primary motives.
   c. biological motives.
   d. homeostasis.

10. Experiments have shown that monkeys will work quite hard to peer through a "window" at such things as model trains going around. What BEST explains why they will do this?
    a. it satisfies a homeostatic drive
    b. it provides novel stimulation
    c. the Yerkes-Dodson law
    d. a biological incentive

11. Which theory proposes that behavior may be aimed at increasing or decreasing alertness and activity depending on the circumstances?
    a. optimal level of arousal
    b. Yerkes-Dodson law
    c. James-Lange theory
    d. novel stimulation theory

12. Which of the following situations is a clear violation of optimal level of arousal theory?
    a. A tired new mother takes a relaxing bath while her child cries.
    b. An overburdened student starts a new job during finals week.
    c. An anxiety-ridden secretary decides to change jobs.
    d. A stressed executive watches a movie during lunch break.

13. Which of the following is the idea that you might be rejected by others if you have a successful career?
    a. fear of success
    b. fear of failure
    c. frustration-aggression theory
    d. opponent-process theory

14. Women who set low goals for themselves because they fear social rejection will most likely
    a. not fear success.
    b. have a fear of failure.
    c. have low *n Ach* scores.
    d. have high *n Ach* scores.

15. The observations that "states of positive feelings are often followed by contrasting negative feelings" and that "any feeling experienced several times loses some of its intensity" are relevant to which theory?
    a. James-Lange
    b. Schachter-Singer
    c. cognitive-enhancement
    d. opponent-process

16. Which of the following is the opponent-process theory is particularly good at explaining?
    a. motives that are difficult to understand
    b. how primary motives are learned
    c. the motivation for novel stimulation
    d. how people become self-actualized

17. Internal desires to do good just for the sake of doing good is evidence of _____ motivation.
    a. competence
    b. incentive
    c. extrinsic
    d. intrinsic

18. Which of the following is an example of intrinsic motivation?
    a. coming home early to avoid punishment
    b. working hard to make much money
    c. playing sports because you love to
    d. achieving goals because others want you to

19. The lowest or most basic needs in Maslow's classification system are called _____ needs.
    a. biological
    b. safety
    c. social
    d. self-esteem

20. According to Maslow's needs hierarchy, what motives will be most prominent in a person's behavior?
    a. self-actualization motives
    b. social and self-esteem motives
    c. primary drives that are easily attained
    d. the lowest, unsatisfied motives

21. How many basic emotions have psychologists agreed upon?
    a. four
    b. six
    c. nine
    d. twelve

22. Most definitions of emotion include the element of
    a. physiological arousal.
    b. drive state.
    c. unconscious thought.
    d. transcendence.

23. The James-Lange theory of emotion states that we
    a. think before we act.
    b. act before we feel.
    c. think before we feel.
    d. feel before we think.

24. Which theory of emotion supports the belief that the experience of an emotion occurs simultaneously with bodily arousal?
    a. opponent-process
    b. James-Lange
    c. Cannon-Bard
    d. facial feedback

25. What does the polygraph device actually measure?
    a. changes in sympathetic arousal
    b. changes in brain activity
    c. whether a person is lying
    d. the degree of guilt a person feels

26. During a polygraph session, if an individual is asked questions that only the person who committed the crime would know the answer to, then what test is being used?
    a. criminal detection
    b. reverse con
    c. subterfuge
    d. guilty knowledge

27. Psychologists who study emotions agree that basic emotions are
    a. learned through experience.
    b. learned through classical conditioning.
    c. learned through modeling.
    d. not learned but are inborn.

28. Research has shown that people who have been blind since birth exhibit the same facial expressions for basic emotions as people who are not blind. This evidence suggests that some emotional expressions are
    a. learned.
    b. innate.
    c. conditioned.
    d. generated.

29. Aggression brought on whenever you are blocked from attaining a goal or desired result defines
    a. catharsis.
    b. cathexis.
    c. frustration.
    d. projectionism.

30. A belief that engaging in competitive sports or watching violent sports can lead to a reduction of violent behavior is compatible with
    a. social learning theory.
    b. frustration-aggression theory.
    c. Freud's instinct theory.
    d. Bandura's theory of aggression.

31. Evidence that violent behavior is learned and passed down from generation to generation has been explained by the fact that
    a. white males living in the North are more violent than those in the South.
    b. rates of homicide among white males in the North are three times higher than in the South.
    c. more recent American immigrants who settled the West tended to be nonviolent.
    d. homicide among white males in the South is three times higher than in New England.

32. According to Staub, what is the key reason why youths join violent gangs?
    a. authoritative-indulgent parenting
    b. low socioeconomic status
    c. feeling of ethnic pride
    d. rejection by parents and peers

Chapter 9 Answer Key

1. c	6. c	11. a	16. a	21. b	26. d	31. d
2. b	7. d	12. b	17. d	22. a	27. d	32. d
3. c	8. c	13. a	18. c	23. d	28. b	
4. b	9. a	14. c	19. a	24. c	29. c	
5. c	10. b	15. d	20. d	25. a	30. c	

10 GENDER & SEXUALITY

LEARNING OBJECTIVES

1. Distinguish among the definitions of sex, gender, and sexual orientation.
2. Distinguish between gender identity and gender role.
3. Recognize the results of research regarding gender similarities and gender differences.
4. Compare and contrast the psychoanalytic and social learning theories of gender identity.
5. Identify characteristics associated with different sexual orientations and recognize the results of research regarding the origins of sexual orientation.
6. Recognize the controversies regarding the admission of openly homosexual men and women into the military.
7. Identify the efforts of those who pioneered the scientific study of sexual behavior.
8. Identify the anatomic structures and functions of male and female sexual anatomy.
9. Identify and understand the stages of the human sexual response cycle.
10. Compare sexual motivation with other primary motives.
11. Recognize the relationship between hormones and sexual behavior.
12. Recognize the patterns of sexual behavior identified by the University of Chicago survey.
13. Distinguish between transvestism and transsexualism.
14. Identify the patterns of sexual behavior called fetishism, sexual sadism, sexual masochism, voyeurism, and exhibitionism.
15. Distinguish between the different types of forced sexual behavior.
16. Define sexual dysfunction and identify common sexual dysfunctions.
17. Identify behaviors that decrease the risk of cancers of the sexual anatomy.
18. Identify sexually transmitted diseases and understand the four general types of infectious agents that cause STDs.
19. Recognize how AIDs is transmitted, know the misperceptions related to AIDs, and identify ways to prevent the spread of STDs.

SAMPLE QUESTIONS

1. When psychologists use the word gender they are referring to the
   a. political ramifications of being male or female.
   b. psychological experience of being male or female.
   c. biological indications contributed by genetics.
   d. hereditary contributions to sexual orientation.

2. One's own view of whether one is male or female is known as
   a. a sexual stereotype.
   b. a gender role.
   c. one's gender identity.
   d. one's sex role.

3. Emotional expressiveness, dependence, and nurturance are traditional feminine
   a. gender identities.
   b. gender roles.
   c. sexual orientations.
   d. sexual behaviors.

4. The most important determinant of a person's gender identity is the
   a. type of hormones present during the prenatal period.
   b. type of hormones present at puberty.
   c. way the person is reared.
   d. nature of the person's first sexual encounter.

5. Which of the following statements regarding the psychological characteristics of males and females best reflects the conclusions drawn from gender research?
   a. Females average much higher scores in mathematical reasoning than do males.
   b. Males average twice as high in mathematical reasoning scores than do females.
   c. When differences in cognitive abilities between the sexes do occur it is most likely due to biological sex.
   d. There are more gender similarities in cognitive abilities than gender differences.

6. When differences in specific cognitive abilities are reported, they appear to be MORE related to
   a. biological sex.
   b. gender.
   c. androgyny.
   d. genetic differences.

7. At what age do girls and boys develop a stable concept of gender role?
   a. 2 to 3 years
   b. 4 to 5 years
   c. 6 to 7 years
   d. 8 to 10 years

8. According to identification theory, why does a child adopt the gender role of its same-sex parent?
   a. to avoid rejection
   b. to mimic adult behavior
   c. to learn appropriate behaviors
   d. to form a sexual identity

9. Homosexual and heterosexual are terms that distinguish
   a. what sex you are.
   b. sexual orientation.
   c. sexual identity.
   d. gender identity.

10. What did the study conducted by the University of Chicago conclude about homosexuality in America?
    a. about 19% of the population reported homosexual behavior
    b. more men than women report same-sex experiences
    c. women tend to have same-sex experiences at a younger age than men
    d. homosexuals tend to live in less populated areas

11. When comparing job performance of homosexuals and heterosexuals in military service,
    a. homosexuals make better officers.
    b. heterosexuals make better officers.
    c. no differences have been found.
    d. homosexuals lacked leadership skills.

12. Freely admitting homosexuals into the military appears to be more of a problem for
    a. heterosexuals.
    b. lesbians.
    c. gays.
    d. bisexuals.

13. Krafft-Ebing believed that abnormal sexual behavior was the result of
    a. premarital sex.
    b. dyspareunia.
    c. masturbation.
    d. homosexuality.

14. Masturbation as a normal sexual function was first confirmed by
    a. Masters.
    b. Johnson.
    c. Kinsey.
    d. Ellis.

15. During the menstrual cycle, the inner lining of the _____ is shed.
    a. fallopian tubes
    b. uterus
    c. vagina
    d. cervix

16. At the time of ovulation, the ova are transported from the ovaries to the _____ via the _____.
    a. uterus; cervix
    b. vulva; clitoris
    c. uterus; fallopian tubes
    d. cervix; vagina

17. Masters and Johnson identified four components of the human sexual response cycle. What are they (in the order that they occur)?
    a. resolution; excitement; orgasmic; plateau
    b. resolution; excitement; plateau; orgasmic
    c. excitement; plateau; orgasmic; resolution
    d. plateau; resolution; excitement; orgasmic

18. When sexual pleasure is very high but not yet at its peak, the person has most likely reached the _____ phase of sexual response.
    a. excitement
    b. orgasmic
    c. refractory
    d. plateau

19. In which of the following ways does sex not resemble the other primary motives?
    a. Initiation of sex is centered in the hypothalamus.
    b. If deprived for long periods, you are more likely to engage in the behavior and may engage in it in increased amounts.
    c. It is not necessary to sustain life.
    d. If you are satisfied and possibly even over-satisfied, a new partner will induce new arousal.

20. In addition to regulating hunger and thirst, which brain structure is involved in the sexual motive?
    a. prostate gland
    b. pineal gland
    c. hippocampus
    d. hypothalamus

21. In many lower animals, sexual motivation is most closely driven by
    a. biological factors.
    b. individual survival.
    c. psychological factors.
    d. level of male estrogen.

22. Compared with nonhuman sexual motives, human sexual motives are
    a. less dependent on hormones.
    b. not affected by hormones.
    c. more dependent on hormones.
    d. just as dependent on hormones.

23. According to the University of Chicago study of sexual behavior, who is having sex the most often?
    a. single men
    b. single women
    c. people in committed relationships
    d. men seeking divorce

24. What percentage of people in committed relationships reported that they receive "great physical pleasure" from sex?
    a. 90 percent
    b. 77 percent
    c. 63 percent
    d. 51 percent

25. Some people obtain sexual satisfaction by dressing as a member of the opposite sex. This practice is called
    a. fetishism.
    b. exhibitionism.
    c. transvestism.
    d. transsexualism.

26. How does a transvestite receive sexual gratification?
    a. by thinking about children in sexual situations
    b. by dressing as a member of the opposite sex
    c. by showing off sexual organs in public
    d. by watching others engaged in sexual acts

27. People who gain sexual pleasure by inflicting pain on others are
    a. masochists.
    b. voyeurs.
    c. sadists.
    d. pedophiles.

28. If a person is a(n) _____, they become sexually aroused by _____.
    a. masochist; inflicting pain
    b. transsexual; inflicting pain
    c. pedophile; exposing genitals
    d. exhibitionist; exposing genitals

29. When a child is involved in the attainment of sexual satisfaction, the abnormal behavior is called
    a. sadomasochism.
    b. pedophilia.
    c. transsexualism.
    d. dyspareunia.

30. Most rapists _____ their victims.
    a. are acquainted with
    b. do not know
    c. murder
    d. sexually desire

31. Any disturbance in the human sexual response cycle is called
    a. a sexual dysfunction.
    b. a sexually transmitted disease.
    c. sexual aversion disorder.
    d. inhibited sexual desire.

32. Milford has a sexual dysfunction. What should his physician rule out as the most common physical cause?
    a. drug abuse
    b. chlamydia
    c. gonorrhea
    d. herpes

33. When should breast self-examinations be performed by women who are still in their child bearing years?
    a. at the end of each menstrual cycle
    b. at least once a year
    c. during their menstrual period
    d. during ovulation

34. Testicular cancers are most common in which age group?
    a. 16 to 35
    b. 27 to 39
    c. 32 to 47
    d. 37 to 65

35. Which of the following is an example of a sexually transmitted disease?
    a. paraphilia
    b. chlamydia
    c. exhibitionism
    d. vaginismus

36. During which stage of syphilis does the victim develop a chancre?
    a. tertiary
    b. primary
    c. viral
    d. febrile

37. A person with the HIV infection _____ AIDS.
    a. cannot ever get
    b. absolutely does have
    c. might have
    d. absolutely does not have

38. How does the HIV virus effect the body?
    a. It directly attacks the cells of the central nervous system.
    b. It directly suppresses respiratory and heart functioning.
    c. It blocks the action of the autonomic nervous system.
    d. It suppresses the bodies immune response.

Chapter 10 Answer Key

1. b	6. b	11. c	16. c	21. a	26. b	31. a	36. b
2. c	7. c	12. a	17. c	22. a	27. c	32. a	37. c
3. b	8. a	13. c	18. d	23. c	28. d	33. a	38. d
4. c	9. b	14. c	19. c	24. a	29. b	34. a	
5. d	10. b	15. b	20. d	25. c	30. a	35. b	

11 PERSONALITY, ASSESSMENT, & INDIVIDUAL DIFFERENCES

LEARNING OBJECTIVES

1. Define the term personality.
2. Distinguish among Freud's concepts of conscious mind, the preconscious mind, and the unconscious mind as part of his psychoanalytic theory.
3. Distinguish among the id, ego, and superego in Freud's psychoanalytic theory.
4. Distinguish among the processes Freud referred to as displacement, sublimation, and identification.
5. List and understand Freud's five psychosexual stages of development.
6. Understand Jung's theory of the mind; distinguish between extroversion and introversion and between personal unconscious and the collective unconscious.
7. Recognize the roles of inferiority feelings, social interest, and goals in Adler's personality theory.
8. Understand the role of anxious insecurity in the personality theory of Horney; recognize Horney's criticisms of Freud's view of women.
9. Understand Bandura's social learning theory, including the roles of cognition in personality development.
10. Identify the basic concepts of humanistic theory, including inner-directedness and subjectivity.
11. Distinguish between the "self" and the "ideal self" and understand the importance of congruence and conditions of worth in Roger's personality theory.
12. Identify the characteristics of a self-actualized person according to Maslow.
13. Compare and contrast humanistic, psychoanalytic, and social learning theories of personality.
14. Distinguish among Allport's cardinal, central, secondary, and common traits, and compare Allport's approach with Cattell's trait theory.
15. List and understand the "big five" personality traits.
16. Recognize the alternative explanations to trait theories called situationism and interactionism.
17. Understand how interviews and observational methods are used to assess personality.
18. Understand how projective tests are used and distinguish between the TAT and the Rorschach inkblot test.
19. Know how objective tests are administered such as the MMPI-2.
20. Recognize the usefulness and accuracy of personality tests.

SAMPLE QUESTIONS

1. The sum total of all the ways of acting, thinking, and feeling that are typical for a person and make that person different from all others is known as
   a. somatotype.
   b. ego.
   c. personality.
   d. subjective self.

2. Which of the following is the best definition of personality as a psychologist would study it?
   a. the typical traits and qualities that make people different from each other
   b. relatively permanent changes in behavior due to experience
   c. the organization of sensation into a meaningful interpretation
   d. the pleasantness or sociabilities of an individual

3. In Freudian theory, primitive and instinctual motives as well as memories and emotions that are so threatening to the conscious mind that they have been repressed, are stored in the
   a. subconscious.
   b. unconscious.
   c. preconscious.
   d. primal conscious.

4 What major contribution did Sigmund Freud offer to the theories of personality development?
   a. people are largely the products of their environments
   b. much of people's behavior is unconsciously determined
   c. most human behaviors are acquired through operant conditioning
   d. social crises are a primary cause of mental illness

5. Cartoons sometimes depict personal conflict by showing the individual being caught between an internal devil tendency and an internal angel tendency. This devil tendency corresponds to the
   a. id.
   b. ego.
   c. superego.
   d. preconscious.

6. Suzy was reared in a home where high moral principles dominated. She attended Sunday school and church since early childhood. In high school, her boyfriend talked her into "sleeping" with him. Which Freudian structure won in this scenario?
   a. superego
   b. reality principle
   c. ego
   d. id

7. To prevent itself from being overwhelmed by excessive demands from the id and superego, the ego relies on
   a. the Oedipus complex.
   b. defense mechanisms.
   c. the reality principle.
   d. the pleasure principle.

8. Seven-year-old Erika got mad at her school teacher but could not express her anger at her teacher. After school, she took out her frustration on her four-year-old brother Jeff. In Freud's view, Erika exhibited signs of
    a. projection.
    b. sublimation.
    c. displacement.
    d. repression.

9. Freud believed that an individual's personality might become stuck in the patterns of an earlier psychosexual stage. He referred to this type of person as being
    a. fixated.
    b. repressed.
    c. displaced.
    d. sublimated.

10. The psychosexual stage that extends from birth to one year is called the _____ stage.
    a. oral
    b. anal
    c. phallic
    d. latency

11. Jung thought that personality could be explained in terms of the two opposing conditions of
    a. extroversion and introversion.
    b. intrinsic motivation and extrinsic motivation.
    c. heredity and environment.
    d. conscious motivation and unconscious motivation.

12. If your friend begins talking about your personality, about whether you are an extrovert or an introvert, and about how your collective and personal unconscious are directing your life, you should suspect that she has been reading
    a. Jung.
    b. Adler.
    c. Freud.
    d. Maslow.

13. According to Adler, striving for superiority would be MOST healthy when it includes
    a. conscious awareness.
    b. the social interest of others.
    c. self deprecation.
    d. reciprocal determination.

14. A basic theme in Adler's personality development theory is that we grow up in a world with bigger, stronger, wiser, and more powerful adults. Due to this, all children experience
    a. the Oedipal conflict.
    b. oral fixation.
    c. feelings of inferiority.
    d. regressive motivation.

15. Among those who have revised Freud's psychoanalytic theory, who has been the MOST influential?
    a. Karen Horney
    b. Alfred Adler
    c. John Watson
    d. Albert Bandura

16. Penis envy is to power envy as
    a. Jung is to Freud.
    b. Jung is to Adler.
    c. Horney is to Adler.
    d. Freud is to Horney.

17. The theory of personality that stresses the functions of reinforcement and imitation is the _____ theory.
    a. psychoanalytic
    b. humanistic
    c. social learning
    d. existential

18. According to social learning theorists, what are the key concepts in the study of personality?
    a. fixation, regression, and defense mechanisms
    b. need fulfillment and self-actualization
    c. the conflict between the person and the environment
    d. classical conditioning, operant conditioning, and modeling

19. Which type of personality theory is called the "third force" and is the least defined of the major approaches to personality?
    a. behaviorism
    b. humanistic theory
    c. psychoanalysis
    d. social learning theory

20. If you believed in humanistic personality theories, which of the following would you be most inclined to agree with?
    a. Humans are pleasure-seeking creatures driven by lust, vengeance, and greed.
    b. Each person is unique and strives to be valued for who they are.
    c. Human beings have no basic qualities. They are shaped by the environment.
    d. Each person is an individual and strives to develop the qualities that promote survival.

21. According to humanistic psychologists, the person we wish to be known as is our
    a. self-concept.
    b. ego ideal.
    c. actualized self.
    d. ideal self.

22. Maladjustment is seen by Rogers as the result of
    a. a discrepancy between the ideal and the real selves.
    b. rejection and fear of certain ego ideals.
    c. faulty reinforcement determinations.
    d. poor childhood experiences.

23. According to Maslow, people can fulfill their potential if they can overcome the complications of everyday life. The tendency to achieve fullest potential is called
    a. the hierarchy of needs.
    b. self-actualization.
    c. existential confrontation.
    d. individualized identity.

24. Having more concern about the welfare of friends, family members and humanity rather than self is an important aspect of
    a. self-efficacy.
    b. self-construct theory.
    c. self-actualization.
    d. selfishness.

25. A prosecutor in a rape trial argues that the defendant has never learned to control his basic animal urges and has failed to develop a conscience because of ineffective parental controls. This description is most compatible with
    a. psychoanalytic theory.
    b. social learning theory.
    c. humanistic theory.
    d. existential theory.

26. The theory of personality most compatible with the view that the basic qualities of personality are shaped by environmental forces is _____ theory.
    a. Freudian
    b. trait
    c. humanistic
    d. social learning

27. Distinctive combinations of personal characteristics are described by _____ theorists.
    a. constitutional
    b. trait
    c. social learning
    d. behavioral

28. While social learning theory is interested in _____ of personality, trait theories are interested in _____ of personality.
    a. developing traits; developing explanations
    b. describing the nature; explaining the origins
    c. explaining the origins; describing the nature
    d. the self-concept; other people's concept

29. Opposing adjectives are used to describe each trait in _____ of personality.
    a. the five-factor model
    b. Cattell's theory
    c. Allport's theory
    d. the situational mode

30. Mary reported that she was sociable, fun-loving, affectionate, talkative, and a joiner when she took a personality test. Mary would be described as high in
    a. conscientiousness.
    b. neuroticism.
    c. extraversion.
    d. agreeableness.

31. Those who believe people behave consistently under certain situations oppose trait theories. These psychologists advocate
    a. self-efficacy.
    b. Allport's theory.
    c. identification.
    d. situationism.

32. According to the person × situation interactionism view, each person behaves _____ in varying situations and are _____ more by some situations than by others.
    a. cautiously; frightened
    b. neurotically; made anxious
    c. differently; influenced
    d. similarly; not influenced

33. The personality assessment tool that is used the most is the
    a. observational method.
    b. thematic apperception test.
    c. interview.
    d. projective test.

34. What is a problem you should be aware of regarding interviews?
    a. They may be structured.
    b. They often only examine typical behaviors.
    c. They are naturalistic.
    d. They are subjective.

35. The Rorschach inkblot test is an example of a(n) _____ personality test.
    a. new
    b. objective
    c. projective
    d. abnormal

36. What is a person asked to do when taking the Rorschach inkblot test?
    a. make up complete stories about pictures
    b. answer a series of true-false questions
    c. describe what they see in an ambiguous picture
    d. draw a picture of a house, tree, and person

37. Objective personality assessment is to projective personality assessment as
    a. Rorschach is to TAT.
    b. MMPI is to TAT.
    c. Rorschach is to MMPI.
    d. TAT is to Rorschach.

38. How are the results of objective personality tests assessed?
    a. trained analysts interpret the results
    b. observers rate answers on a 5 point scale
    c. results are compared to other test takers
    d. correct answers were established by behaviorists

39. Which of the following is a major criticism of personality tests?
    a. cost
    b. time constraints
    c. objectivity
    d. accuracy

40. Which of the following is TRUE of projective tests?
    a. good at predicting behavior
    b. unsuccessful in distinguishing people with psychological problems
    c. good at detecting psychiatric disorders
    d. very inexpensive to administer and very easy to learn to administer

Chapter 11 Answer Key

1. c	6. d	11. a	16. d	21. d	26. d	31. d	36. c
2. a	7. b	12. a	17. c	22. a	27. b	32. c	37. b
3. b	8. c	13.b	18. d	23. b	28. c	33. c	38. c
4. b	9.a	14. c	19. b	24. c	29. a	34. d	39. d
5. a	10.a	15. a	20. b	25. a	30. c	35. c	40. b

12 STRESS, HEALTH, & COPING

LEARNING OBJECTIVES

1. Define stress, list the sources of stress and understand health psychology's interest in stress.
2. Distinguish among the following types of conflict: approach-approach, avoidance-avoidance, approach-avoidance, and multiple approach-avoidance.
3. Understand the relationship between life events and stress.
4. Understand the two insights about stress reactions, know the stages of Selye's general adaptation syndrome, and recognize the healthy and unhealthy aspects of the general adaptation syndrome.
5. Understand the relationship between stress and the immune system.
6. List and understand five major factors that influence reactions to stress.
7. Recognize cognitive factors in stress reactions and distinguish between sensitizers and repressors.
8. Identify the characteristics of the Type A personality and know the relationship between Type A personality and heart disease.
9. List and understand three effective methods of coping with stress.
10. List and understand three ineffective methods of coping with stress.
11. Distinguish among the major defense mechanisms.
12. Understand how progressive relaxation training is used to prevent health problems.
13. Know how eating right, exercising, and medical compliance affect health.
14. Understand how health practices affect mortality and recognize the potential benefits of psychology to health.

SAMPLE QUESTIONS

1. The area in psychology that studies factors surrounding health, lifestyles, and health care is called _____ psychology.
    a. medical
    b. lifespan
    c. fitness
    d. health

2   You enjoyed your general psychology course so much that you decided to register for more psychology courses next semester. However, you are among the last to register and all the desirable psychology courses are already filled. The stress you are feeling is the result of
    a. frustration.
    b. conflict.
    c. pressure.
    d. personality inadequacy.

3. Jane is experiencing stress. Both of her boyfriends have asked her out for the same night. Assuming she is equally attracted to both, which source of stress is Jane experiencing?
    a. approach-avoidance conflict
    b. approach-approach conflict
    c.   avoidance-avoidance conflict
    d. frustration-pressure conflict

4. You love both psychology and sociology and are having trouble deciding which one should be your major. You are in the midst of an _____ conflict.
    a. approach-approach
    b. avoidance-avoidance
    c. frustration
    d. vacillation

5. Research on the relationship between stress and environmental conditions such as noise, humidity, and air pollution has shown that
    a. such conditions can increase psychological problems.
    b. there is no significant relationship.
    c. the physical rather than the psychological problems show a relationship.
    d. not enough research has been done to draw a conclusion.

6. Regarding positive and negative life events, which of the following is true?
    a. Positive life events always offset the stressful effects of negative life events.
    b. Positive life events can create stress.
    c. Stressful life events always produce pressure.
    d. Stressful life events always produce tension.

7. Selye's three-stage pattern of reaction to stress is known as the
    a. Personality Adjustment System.
    b. Social Readjustment Scale.
    c. General Adaptation Syndrome.
    d. Stress Coping Pattern.

8. What are the stages, in order, of the general adaptation syndrome?
    a. alarm, resistance, and avoidance
    b. avoidance, resistance, and exhaustion
    c. avoidance, exhaustion, and adaptation
    d. alarm, resistance, and exhaustion

9. What is the body's natural disease-fighting system called?
   a. suppression system
   b. immune system
   c. autonomic system
   d. parasympathetic system

10. Cancer patients showed increases in immune system functioning after
    a. they were questioned about life events.
    b. stress management treatment.
    c. the general adaptation syndrome began.
    d. they were taught repressor coping styles.

11. A college senior is more likely to know how to handle examination stress and therefore will be under less stress than an incoming freshman. This illustrates which of the following factors that influence reactions to stress?
    a. predictability and control
    b. prior experience with stress
    c. social support
    d. physiological factors producing stress

12. In a study, autonomic arousal was measured while one group received electric shock 95 percent of the time, a second received electric shock 50 percent of the time, and a third received electric shock 5 percent of the time. The group that was shocked 5 percent of the time showed the most arousal due to the influence of what factor?
    a. increased withdrawal
    b. increased conflict
    c. lowered predictability
    d. lowered immune functioning

13. A friend related a story about her cousin who just died of cancer. She told you that her cousin had a cough for two years before she finally took friends' advice and saw a physician. Your friend's cousin was probably
    a. a Type A personality.
    b. an intellectualizer.
    c. a sensitizer.
    d. a repressor.

14. Research on repression and sensitization indicates that
    a. sensitizers have more effective coping strategies.
    b. repressors have more effective coping strategies.
    c. neither strategy is really more effective, just different.
    d. each coping strategy is effective depending on the situation.

15. Psychologists have identified a hard-driving, achievement-oriented, coronary-prone personality pattern. This pattern is referred to as
    a. Type A personality.
    b. dissonant personality.
    c. "hot" personality.
    d. sensitizer personality.

16. John is widely regarded as a workaholic. He has not had a day off in the last five years and goes to work even when he is ill. On most days, he is driven to produce at least twice as much as anyone else. John's pattern of behavior is consistent with
    a. a repressor personality.
    b. a sensitizer personality.
    c. Type A personality.
    d. double avoidance personality.

17. Removing stress from your life is one method of
    a. effective coping.
    b. ineffective coping.
    c. an aversion mechanism.
    d. avoidance coping.

18. After being promoted to department head, Bill found the job to be uncomfortable and highly stressful. Ultimately, Bill resigned from the position and returned to his former job, where he reported being much happier. Which method of coping with stress did Bill use?
    a. managing stress reactions, an effective coping method
    b. withdrawal, an ineffective coping method
    c. removing stress, an effective coping method
    d. excessive use of defense mechanisms, an ineffective coping method

19. Effective coping involves _____, whereas ineffective coping involves _____.
    a. removing the source of stress; withdrawing from the stress
    b. defense mechanisms; managing stress reactions
    c. aggression; frustration
    d. repression; sensitization

20. People sometimes respond to frustration by trying to ignore it or to escape from it. This tendency is referred to as
    a. sublimation.
    b. reaction formation.
    c. suppression.
    d. withdrawal.

21. According to Freud, defense mechanisms are used to
    a. assure that the id is gratified.
    b. control the anxiety of the ego.
    c. protect the superego from the ego.
    d. protect the ego from the superego.

22. Jennifer sees her own shortcomings and wicked desires in the behaviors of others. She is using which defense mechanism?
    a. regression
    b. rationalization
    c. reaction formation
    d. projection

23. To use progressive relaxation training, you must first know the difference between _____ and _____.
    a. muscle; fat
    b. mind; behavior
    c. stress; aggression
    d. tense muscle; relaxed muscle

24. Progressive relaxation training has been found to be helpful in which of the following areas?
    a. hypothermia
    b. low blood pressure
    c. insomnia
    d. uremia

25.   Which of the following leads to high levels of blood cholesterol when eaten in excess?
       a.   vegetables
       b.   fiber
       c.   salt
       d.   red meat

26.   Polly wants to eat right to improve her health. Which of the following would you recommend?
       a.   lower intake of salt
       b.   lower weight and don't worry about cholesterol
       c.   cut down on consumption of fiber
       d.   depend on medication to lower cholesterol

27.   Compared to an experimental group that engaged in 6 to 7 positive health practices, what was the death rate for the group that engaged in 0 to 3 positive health practices?
       a.   10 percent higher
       b.   20 percent higher
       c.   50 percent higher
       d.   70 percent higher

28.   How can health psychologists help with the rising cost of health care?
       a.   disease prevention
       b.   developing direct billing practices
       c.   by starting HMOs
       d.   by teaching Type A coping traits

Chapter 12 Answer Key

1. d	6. b	11. b	16. c	21. b	26. a
2. a	7. c	12. c	17. a	22. d	27. c
3. b	8. d	13.d	18. c	23. d	28. a
4. a	9.b	14. d	19. a	24. c	
5. a	10.b	15. a	20. d	25. d	

13 PSYCHOLOGICAL DISORDERS & ABNORMAL BEHAVIOR

LEARNING OBJECTIVES

1. Define abnormal behavior and distinguish between the continuity hypothesis and the discontinuity hypothesis.
2. Recognize how abnormal behavior was viewed differently throughout history, including supernatural theories, biological theories, and psychological theories.
3. Define insanity and understand how and when the term is used.
4. Distinguish among specific phobia, social phobia, and agoraphobia.
5. Distinguish between generalized anxiety disorder and panic anxiety disorder.
6. Recognize the causes and effects of posttraumatic stress disorder.
7. Recognize the differences between obsessions and compulsions.
8. Identify the following somatoform disorders: somatization disorders, hypochondriasis, conversion disorders, and pain disorders.
9. Distinguish between dissociative amnesia and dissociative fugue.
10. Recognize the symptoms of depersonalization and dissociative identity disorder.
11. Identify the characteristics of mood disorders including major depression and bipolar affective disorder.
12. Recognize the importance of cognitive factors in depression and know the results of research into postpartum depression.
13. Recognize the three types of problems that characterize schizophrenia.
14. Distinguish among the following types of schizophrenia: paranoid schizophrenia, disorganized schizophrenia, and catatonic schizophrenia.
15. Identify the characteristics of delusional disorder and recognize how it differs from schizophrenia.
16. Identify the characteristics of the personality disorders, including schizoid personality disorder and antisocial personality disorder.

SAMPLE QUESTIONS

1. Which hypothesis states that abnormal behavior is similar to normal behavior but is a more severe and harmful form of it?
    a. continuity
    b. psychoanalytic
    c. discontinuity
    d. medical

2. Why is it so difficult to define abnormal behavior?
    a. psychologists have no standardized diagnostic criteria
    b. rarely are abnormal behaviors clearly distinguishable
    c. it involves subjective judgements
    d. supernatural components are involved

3. The viewpoint that considers the causes of psychological disorders as stemming from bacterial infections or physical problems is known as the _____ viewpoint.
    a. humanistic
    b. psychoanalytic
    c. neuropsychiatric
    d. biological

4. Treatment for the disorder known as paresis was important in advancing the _____ theory of abnormal behavior.
    a. supernatural
    b. biological
    c. psychological
    d. interpersonal

5. The term insanity
    a. is not a psychological term.
    b. is the same as psychosis.
    c. has no usefulness.
    d. is used only in clinical psychology.

6. When the term insanity is used to determine whether or not a person should stand trial, it is used in the context of
    a. criminality.
    b. commitment.
    c. medicine.
    d. competence.

7. If an individual has excessive problems with nervousness, tension, worry, and fright, he or she may be suffering from a(n)
    a. paresis.
    b. anxiety disorder.
    c. paranoid reaction.
    d. conversion disorder.

8. Larry's mother did not enjoy going to the mall. Whenever she went she invariably asked Larry to take her home within ten minutes. One day Larry wanted to stay and insisted that she wait for him. After about ten more minutes his mother reported feeling a smothering and choking sensation, like she was trapped and could not get enough air. Her symptoms are probably the result of
    a. an obsessive disorder.
    b. a conversion disorder.
    c. a compulsive disorder.
    d. a phobic disorder.

9. Brittany seems to be in a continuous state of anxiety, but she is unable to identify the source of her feelings. The most likely diagnosis for Brittany is
    a. generalized anxiety disorder.
    b. simple phobia.
    c. panic anxiety disorder.
    d. somatoform disorder.

10. Of the disorders listed below, which is a type of anxiety disorder?
    a. conversion disorder
    b. fugue
    c. panic disorder
    d. learned helplessness

11. Flashbacks, feelings of guilt over their survival, and pervasive tenseness are characteristic of persons suffering from
    a. IV drug use.
    b. a phobic disorder.
    c. posttraumatic stress disorder.
    d. obsessive-compulsive disorder.

12. Brad has been reliving his war experiences since he left Vietnam over 20 years ago. In addition, he is frequently tense and feels a deep sense of guilt that he made it home. The MOST likely diagnosis is
    a. generalized anxiety disorder.
    b. dissociative disorder.
    c. posttraumatic stress disorder.
    d. histrionic personality disorder.

13. Which of the following must be present for a diagnosis of obsessive-compulsive disorder?
    a. anxiety-provoking thoughts that will not go away
    b. memory loss for at least 1 week
    c. physical symptoms with no known cause
    d. major mood swings that last up to 6 weeks

14. Which of the following pairs is correct?
    a. obsessions: behaviors
    b. obsessions: thoughts
    c. compulsions: cognitions
    d. compulsions: thoughts

15. Disorders in which the individual experiences the symptoms of physical health problems that have psychological rather than physical causes are known as _____ disorders.
    a. dissociation
    b. psychomedical
    c. somatoform
    d. paranoid

16. Mary has been changing doctors frequently and can't understand why none of her doctors can find anything wrong with her. She complains of nausea and tiredness and has recently started taking many different kinds of pills, hoping that something will help. Mary is displaying the characteristics of
    a. conversion disorder.
    b. somatization disorder.
    c. compulsive disorder.
    d. panic attack.

17. Amnesia caused by extensive psychological stress is termed _____ amnesia.
    a. physiogenic
    b. dissociative
    c. retrograde
    d. anterograde

18. Semiconscious wandering is a characteristic of dissociative
    a. fugue.
    b. amnesia.
    c. interference.
    d. recall.

19. When people feel like they are distorted or unreal, this feeling is called
    a. astral projection.
    b. depersonalization.
    c. psychogenic fugue.
    d. major affective disorder.

20. Sarah felt unreal, like a robot. Her hands seemed too large for the rest of her body and they seemed to move of their own free will. She knew that her perceptions were not accurate, but they had an eerie sense of reality to them. Her altered state of consciousness was temporary and could be considered
    a. depersonalization.
    b. a conversion disorder.
    c. psychogenic fugue.
    d. delusional schizophrenia.

21. Mood disorders are characterized by
    a. generalized anxiety and stress.
    b. a splitting of different personalities.
    c. lack of physical symptoms for the disorder.
    d. wide emotional swings.

22. The incidence of major depression is highest in individuals aged
    a. 12 to 16.
    b. 27 to 33.
    c. 45 to 55.
    d. 72 to 78.

23. According to Aaron Beck, a depressed person is more likely to attribute negative events to _____ factors.
    a. external
    b. internal
    c. changing
    d. specific

24. Postpartum depression refers to depression occurring after
    a.   childbirth.
    b.   financial loss.
    c.   the death of a loved one.
    d.   return from war.

25. Schizophrenia is a disorder that affects slightly less than _____ percent of the population.
    a.   1
    b.   4
    c.   9
    d.   15

26. If you could give someone with schizophrenia a drug that would stop them from hearing voices that were not actually present, the drug would eliminate
    a.   delusions.
    b.   proclivities.
    c.   catatonias.
    d.   hallucinations.

27. Delusions of grandeur, delusions of persecution, and hallucinations characterize
    a.   paranoid schizophrenia.
    b.   schizoid personality.
    c.   catatonic schizophrenia.
    d.   schizotypal personality.

28. "I realize that everyone is talking about me, mostly behind my back. Yesterday I read the paper and found that all the reporters were writing specifically about me. I found coded messages in several articles, which of course only I could decipher." Which disorder is the person in question MOST likely to be diagnosed with?
    a.   paranoid schizophrenia
    b.   catatonic schizophrenia
    c.   dissociative disorder
    d.   somatoform disorder

29. Delusional disorders are relatively
    a.   life threatening.
    b.   harmless.
    c.   common.
    d.   rare.

30. How might someone with delusional disorder be distinguished from someone with paranoid schizophrenia?
    a.   The person with delusional disorder does not exhibit catatonia.
    b.   The person with delusional disorder does exhibit catatonia.
    c.   The person with delusional disorder has delusions that are more illogical.
    d.   The person with delusional disorder has delusions that are less illogical.

31. Personality disorders are believed to be the result of which of the following?
    a.   improperly childhood development
    b.   chromosomal damage
    c.   an extremely frightening experience
    d.   classical conditioning

32. Jim was caught again trying to pawn some of his parent's antique jewelry. He skipped so much school that he will have to repeat his courses. He is also unconcerned that he has gotten two different girls pregnant in the past year. He would probably be diagnosed as having a(n)
    a. adventurous adolescent period.
    b. antisocial personality disorder.
    c. schizoid personality disorder.
    d. dependent personality disorder.

Chapter 13 Answer Key

1. a	6. d	11. c	16. b	21. d	26. d	31. a
2. c	7. b	12. c	17. b	22. c	27. a	32. b
3. d	8. d	13. a	18. a	23. b	28. a	
4. b	9. a	14. b	19. b	24. a	29. d	
5. a	10. c	15. c	20. a	25. a	30. d	

14 THERAPIES: TREATMENT OF PSYCHOLOGIAL DISORDERS

LEARNING OBJECTIVES

1. Define and understand how psychotherapy is used to help people.
2. Identify the ethical standards for psychotherapy.
3. Recognize the characteristics of psychoanalysis and identify the techniques of psychoanalytic psychotherapy.
4. Compare and contrast client-centered psychotherapy and Gestalt psychotherapy.
5. Distinguish between the following behavior therapy methods for reducing fear: systematic desensitization and flooding.
6. Recognize the goals and techniques of social skills training, assertiveness training, and aversive conditioning.
7. Recognize the goals of cognitive therapy and identify the maladaptive cognitions that, according to Beck, contribute to depression.
8. Identify the fundamental concepts of feminist psychotherapy.
9. Identify the advantages of group therapy and recognize the goals of family therapy.
10. Recognize when medical therapies are used to treat abnormal behavior and distinguish among drug therapy, electroconvulsive therapy, and psychosurgery.
11. Recognize the goals of community psychology.

SAMPLE QUESTIONS

1. The process used by mental health professionals to help people with psychological problems is known as
    a. behavior therapy.
    b. psychotherapy.
    c. psychoanalytic treatment.
    d. drug therapy.

2. Psychotherapy is a _____ process used by _____.
    a. general; the general public
    b. general; trained professionals
    c. specialized; the general public
    d. specialized; trained professionals

3. What do the goals of treatment, choice of treatment, and voluntary client participation have in common? They are _____ considerations in psychotherapy.
    a. monetary
    b. ethical
    c. cultural
    d. moral

4. The highest ethical standards must be maintained during psychotherapy due to differences in _____ between the therapist and the client.
    a. power
    b. social standing
    c. income
    d. education

5. The underlying belief of psychoanalytic psychotherapy is that emotional problems result from
    a. repressed conflicts.
    b. conscious indecision over major stressors.
    c. excessive sexual activity.
    d. the inability to feel guilt.

6. Which type of therapist would MOST likely use free association and dream analysis to explain unconscious motivations?
    a. feminist therapist
    b. cognitive therapist
    c. psychoanalyst
    d. Gestalt therapist

7. The therapist's principal job in client-centered therapy is to
    a. convey thoughtful interpretations.
    b. create a safe atmosphere.
    c. be critical of the patient's irrational beliefs.
    d. develop a conditional therapeutic situation.

8. Client-centered therapy is a form of _____ therapy.
    a. cognitive-behavioral
    b. psychodynamic
    c. Gestalt
    d. humanistic

9. An approach to therapy that emphasizes the learning of new skills is the
   a. Gestalt approach.
   b. cognitive approach.
   c. behavioral approach.
   d. client-centered approach.

10. Rita's therapist believes the best way to treat her phobia is through relearning. The therapist describes several possible techniques that might be attempted, including counterconditioning, reinforcement therapy, and modeling. Rita's therapist is most likely trained in _____ therapy.
    a. psychoanalytical
    b. Gestalt
    c. behavior
    d. client-centered

11. A therapist guided her client to perform new behaviors by giving instructions and demonstrations. The therapist MOST likely used
    a. social skills training.
    b. cognitive therapy.
    c. psychoanalytic therapy.
    d. humanistic therapy.

12. A behavioral therapist may have a client watch people perform a desired behavior so that the client will learn the desired behavior or at least know what it is. This is a form of
    a. classical conditioning.
    b. systematic desensitization.
    c. social skills training.
    d. extinction therapy.

13. According to Ellis and Beck, people become psychologically disturbed because they
    a. learn maladaptive behaviors.
    b. are unaware of unconscious conflicts.
    c. have maladaptive ways of thinking.
    d. are aware of their irrational beliefs.

14. If you have a friend in psychotherapy and she begins talking about how she is trying to stop making arbitrary inferences about her interactions with people, her therapist was MOST likely influenced by
    a. Perls.
    b. Beck.
    c. Rogers.
    d. Wolpe.

15. Which of the following is TRUE regarding feminist psychotherapy?
    a. It is only for women.
    b. It fosters independence.
    c. It encourages traditional roles.
    d. It is not accepted by other psychotherapies.

16. Michele recently went back to work after spending twelve years raising her children at home. She is having some anxiety over the changes in her life. What kind of therapy is geared towards helping people like Michele?
    a. systematic desensitization
    b. in vivo flooding
    c. the systems approach
    d. feminist psychotherapy

17. Which of the following is an advantage to group psychotherapy?
    a. letting other people solve your problems for you
    b. learning that your problems are unique to you
    c. getting more individual attention from the therapist
    d. learning that you are not alone in your problems

18. Mrs. Peterson is having a difficult time interacting with others and making new friends. Which type of therapy might be of MOST benefit to her?
    a. flooding
    b. group therapy
    c. Gestalt therapy
    d. catharsis

19. The most common form of medical therapy is
    a. drug therapy.
    b. ECT.
    c. psychosurgery.
    d. frontal lobotomy.

20. Which drug marked the beginning of the drug therapy movement in 1954 with its success in helping schizophrenic patients?
    a. Librium
    b. Thorazine
    c. Stelazine
    d. lithium

21. An approach that views the treatment of mental disturbance as an interaction between individuals and the area in which they live and includes the use of paraprofessionals and halfway houses is known as
    a. milieu therapy.
    b. community mental health.
    c. deinstitutionalization.
    d. paraprofessional therapy.

22. The prevention of serious psychological disturbances is the goal of
    a. counselors.
    b. social workers.
    c. community psychologists.
    d. behavioral psychiatry.

Chapter 14 Answer Key

1. b	6. c	11. a	16. d	21. b
2. d	7. b	12. c	17. d	22. c
3. b	8. d	13. c	18. b	
4. a	9. c	14. b	19. a	
5. a	10. c	15. b	20. b	

15 SOCIAL PSYCHOLOGY

LEARNING OBJECTIVES

1. Define social psychology.
2. Understand the attribution process and distinguish between the fundamental attribution error and the self-serving bias.
3. Recognize how groups can contribute to deindividuation and identify the conditions and steps a bystander makes in the decision whether to help or not help.
4. Distinguish among social loafing, social facilitation, and social impairment.
5. Recognize how polarization and groupthink affect group problem solving.
6. Define conformity and know the factors that have been found to increase conformity.
7. Understand the importance of Zimbardo's prison study and recognize the role of social roles and social norms.
8. Define obedience and understand the significance of Milgram's research on obedience.
9. Identify the components of attitudes and know the origins of attitudes.
10. Recognize how characteristics of the speaker, the message, and the listener affect persuasion.
11. Identify techniques used in persuasion.
12. Recognize the role of cognitive dissonance in behavior and attitude change.
13. Understand the relationship between prejudice and stereotypes and recognize how stereotypes affect our attributions about other people's behavior.
14. Distinguish among the explanations for why prejudice arises and identify some effective antidotes for combating prejudice.
15. Understand the factors involved in person perception, including negative information, primacy effects, emotions, and attribution processes.
16. Identify the general factors that influence attraction, including proximity, similar and complementary characteristics, competence, physical attractiveness, mutual liking, and gender differences.
17. Identify the roles played by expectations and equity in maintaining relationships.

SAMPLE QUESTIONS

1. Social psychology is primarily concerned with
   a. brain mechanisms that relate to social behavior.
   b. social learning theory.
   c. individuals as they interact with others.
   d. how people perceive events in their environment.

2. Which of the following would MOST likely attract the interest of a social psychologist?
   a. the effect of conformity on prejudiced behavior
   b. the similarities in family structure in various cultures
   c. the social structure of ant colonies
   d. the relationship between brain structure and socially assertive behavior

3. The fact that we constantly try to make sense out of the behavior of ourselves and others is related to which concept?
   a. externalization
   b. attribution
   c. prejudice
   d. intellectualization

4. An athlete responds to a career-threatening injury by persevering through a rigorous rehabilitation program. Those who know this athlete explain his perseverance in terms of his desire to compete and to express his natural talents. The social process underlying this explanation is
   a. social penetration.
   b. dissonance reduction.
   c. attribution.
   d. diffusion of responsibility.

5. When a person can blend into a group and not worry about his or her own personal responsibilities, _____ has occurred.
   a. altruism
   b. normalization
   c. social loafing
   d. deindividuation

6. The individual who joins a lynch mob or a vigilante group almost never has a previous history of violent behavior. This fact demonstrates the powerful effects of
   a. the diffusion of responsibility.
   b. latent aggressive tendencies in people.
   c. group actions upon individuals' behavior.
   d. dispositional attributions.

7. People working in groups will often exert less effort than if they worked alone. This tendency is known as
   a. social inhibition.
   b. social loafing.
   c. social dissonance.
   d. personal inconsistency.

8. The college instructor found that class projects were of poorer quality when three students worked together than when each student did a project. This difference can be explained by the phenomenon of
   a. the sleeper effect.
   b. diffusion of responsibility.
   c. social loafing.
   d. polarization.

9.   The group polarization effect refers to the tendency for
     a.   group members to conform.
     b.   groups to split up into smaller groups.
     c.   members of a group to feel that it is them against the world.
     d.   a group to arrive at extreme decisions.

10. In groupthink, dissenting opinions
     a.   are not expressed.
     b.   are expressed but not welcome.
     c.   tend to be irrationally expressed.
     d.   are welcome but not expressed.

11. The definition of conformity involves the notion of yielding to group pressure
     a.   because of some social threat.
     b.   because of a fear of negative consequences.
     c.   for fear of retribution.
     d.   without a direct request to comply.

12. When others in the group all agree on the same answer, a person is most likely to
     a.   polarize.
     b.   dissent.
     c.   conform.
     d.   disagree.

13. Culturally determined rules and guidelines that tell us how to behave in groups are called
     a.   obedience rules.
     b.   gender roles.
     c.   social roles.
     d.   rules of decorum.

14. Trish appears very professional and hard-working at work. When she is with her family, she kicks back and lets her mother take care of her needs. When she is with friends, she lets loose and jokes and plays interactional games. Trish behaves very differently in each situation due to varying
     a.   levels of conformity.
     b.   social roles.
     c.   degrees of arousal.
     d.   gender rules.

15. Milgram's studies demonstrated that people do what they are told when
     a.   they are under the grip of polarization.
     b.   they are unsure of themselves.
     c.   asked by an authority figure.
     d.   in stressful situations.

16. In Milgram's original study, subjects were ordered to continue giving increasingly painful shocks to a protesting victim. What percentage of subjects went all the way to the "XXX," 450-volt level?
     a.   2 percent
     b.   5 percent
     c.   25 percent
     d.   65 percent

17. According to your text, what are the three components of attitudes?
     a.   social roles, groupthink, polarization
     b.   groupthink, polarization, dispositions
     c.   beliefs, feelings, dispositions
     d.   feelings, emotions, persuasion

18. When a person thinks, feels, and acts toward something in a consistently favorable or unfavorable way, a(n) _____ has developed.
    a. attitude
    b. trait
    c. disposition
    d. attribution

19. The process of changing another person's attitudes through arguments and other related means is called
    a. conformity.
    b. obedience.
    c. persuasion.
    d. attribution.

20. Attitudes are often subject to change if the communicator
    a. delivers a nonemotional message.
    b. uses cognitive dissonance.
    c. is targeting older people.
    d. is credible.

21. Cedric saw an ad for a big screen television at a great price. When he went to the television show room he was told that the model was completely sold out but another similar model was available for a slightly higher price. This is an example of the
    a. low-ball technique.
    b. foot-in-the-door technique.
    c. door-in-the-face technique.
    d. to-good-to-be-true technique.

22. Which technique used in the persuasion of a sale often works even though the buyer gets the worse end of the deal?
    a. foot-in-the-door technique
    b. low-ball technique
    c. to-good-to-be-true technique
    d. buyer-beware technique

23. Which is most likely to change when behavior and attitudes are inconsistent?
    a. Attitudes will often follow behavior.
    b. Behavior will generally change to match attitudes.
    c. Behaviors will generally change in the direction of the attitude and the attitude will change in the direction of the behavior.
    d. Neither will change in most persons.

24. The theory of cognitive dissonance holds that inconsistencies between attitudes and behavior are uncomfortable,
    a. causing people to engage in groupthink.
    b. but attitude change does not reduce dissonance.
    c. and people will therefore change their attitudes to reduce this discomfort.
    d. and so people engage in attribution to reduce the discomfort.

25. The general prejudgment of a person based on inappropriate criteria (such as race or gender) is formally called
    a. racism.
    b. prejudice.
    c. sexism.
    d. discrimination.

26. Bill thinks stereotypically about foreigners, disliking them without making any efforts to know them. Bill is demonstrating
    a.   reactance.
    b.   prejudice.
    c.   dissonance.
    d.   displacement.

27. The realistic conflict theory attempts to explain how _____ arises.
    a.   stereotypes
    b.   prejudice
    c.   obedience
    d.   compliance

28. Jo is very popular at her school and is a leader among her group members. The students who do not follow her lead are considered outsiders. Which explanation of how prejudice arises appears to be at work in this example?
    a.   conflict theory
    b.   us versus them
    c.   obedience theory
    d.   group polarization

29. In the process of person perception, negative information
    a.   tends to leave a stronger impression.
    b.   tends to leave a weak impression.
    c.   is outweighed by positive traits.
    d.   is not as long-lasting as positive information.

30. The enduring quality of initial impressions is termed
    a.   social comparison.
    b.   a prototype.
    c.   the primacy effect.
    d.   the recency effect.

31. It is generally most flattering to be liked by someone who
    a.   holds attitudes similar to yours.
    b.   holds attitudes different from yours.
    c.   resolves dissonance the same way you do.
    d.   you did not like at first.

32. Under which condition do opposites tend to attract?
    a.   under conditions of polarization
    b.   under conditions of deindividuation
    c.   when traits are complementary
    d.   when cognitive dissonance is high

33. In social psychology, equity theory attempts to predict the
    a.   degree of success in maintaining relationships.
    b.   required attribution levels to maintain relationships.
    c.   appropriate balance of predispositional and situational attributions.
    d.   the appropriate balance between primacy and recency factors in a relationship.

34. Desire to have someone near to you and having a deep, caring affection for a person are traits of _____ love.
    a.   passionate
    b.   eros
    c.   romantic
    d.   companionate

Chapter 15 Answer Key

1. c	6. c	11. d	16. d	21. a	26. b	31. b
2. a	7. b	12. c	17. c	22. b	27. b	32. c
3. b	8. c	13. c	18. a	23. a	28. b	33. a
4. c	9. d	14. b	19. c	24. c	29. a	34. d
5. d	10. a	15. c	20. d	25. b	30. c	

16 APPLIED PSYCHOLOGY: BUSINESS & OTHER PROFESSIONS

LEARNING OBJECTIVES

1. Identify the role of industrial-organizational psychologists in the workplace.
2. Identify the types of measures that are commonly used for employee selection and evaluation.
3. Compare the validity of various job selection measures.
4. Recognize the challenges involved in the fair selection of minority employees.
5. Understand the relationship between job satisfaction and productivity; identify the strategies that are designed to improve both.
6. Identify the traits of successful leaders and know the status of women and minorities in leadership positions.
7. Identify the goals of human factors engineering.
8. Know the role of health psychology in the workplace.
9. Recognize how psychology has been applied to employee training, computer-assisted instruction, and advertising and marketing.
10. Identify the role of environmental psychologists in the workplace.
11. Identify the characteristics of defendants and jury members that affect conviction rates.
12. Recognize the importance of psychological factors in presenting evidence and interrogating criminal suspects.
13. Identify the role of educational psychologists in the workplace.
14. Understand the effects of mastery learning and intelligent tutoring systems on children's' education.
15. Recognize the importance of person x situation interaction in the evaluation of new educational approaches and understand how criterion-referenced testing is used in the classroom.
16. Identify the goals of mainstreaming.

SAMPLE QUESTIONS

1. Increasing job satisfaction is a key goal for a(n) _____ psychologist.
   a. industrial-organizational
   b. social-learning
   c. behavioral-business
   d. cognitive-management

2. The application of psychological principles to the world of work is the area of _____ psychology.
   a. employment
   b. industrial-organizational
   c. human factors
   d. business-management

3. The industrial-organizational psychologist typically uses psychological tests and measures
   a. only to select new employees.
   b. only when evaluating current employees.
   c. when selecting new employees and evaluating current employees.
   d. when marketing new products and evaluating sale of old products.

4. You are applying for a job and are waiting to be interviewed. It would be to your best advantage to place yourself in the following sequence:
   a. before a highly-qualified applicant.
   b. before a poorly-qualified applicant.
   c. after a highly-qualified applicant.
   d. after a poorly-qualified applicant.

5. How valid are assessment center evaluations compared to intellectual ability tests?
   a. incredibly more
   b. equally
   c. slightly more
   d. less

6. How well and how quickly new employees understand their job is best predicted by _____ tests.
   a. intelligence
   b. biodata
   c. performance rating
   d. assessment center

7. If 50 percent of white applicants were selected on the basis of an intelligence test, _____ percent of African-Americans applicants would be selected.
   a. 1
   b. 4
   c. 16
   d. 48

8. When a test favors the information and skills from a particular culture, it is said to be
   a. culture specific.
   b. culturally valid.
   c. reliable
   d. biased.

9. If your friend in business says that job satisfaction is high in her plant, which of the following is <u>MOST</u> likely true?
   a. Turnover and absenteeism are low.
   b. Productivity is high.
   c. Quotas are not used.
   d. Profits are extremely low.

10. What is the general relationship between job satisfaction and employee productivity?
    a. They are not directly related.
    b. Job satisfaction causes productivity.
    c. Productivity causes job satisfaction.
    d. They each influence one another.

11. The influence of one group member on the others as they work toward shared goals is called
    a. destructuring.
    b. productivity.
    c. leadership.
    d. social loafing.

12. Charisma, clear vision, inspiration, and personalized attention are traits of
    a. human engineers.
    b. organizational psychologists.
    c. employee selection.
    d. successful leaders.

13. Human factors engineers performed research that suggested that _____ persons are better at handling stressful jobs than others.
    a. introverted
    b. extraverted
    c. flexible
    d. manipulative

14. Investigations by human factors engineers of nuclear power plant accidents have suggested that human error was the result of
    a. complicated visual displays.
    b. outdated equipment.
    c. too many ill workers on the job site.
    d. poor simulated management tasks.

15. Why would an employer be interested in promoting employee health?
    a. Healthy employees file more insurance claims.
    b. Healthy employees are more productive.
    c. Healthy employees show higher rates of turnover.
    d. Healthy employees demand better health plans.

16. Compared to persons who exercise regularly, sedentary persons are at risk for _____ twice as much.
    a. cancer
    b. the common cold
    c. cardiovascular disease
    d. flu

17. How has training new employees been made more efficient for employers?
    a. through mainstreaming
    b. by using Project Follow Through
    c. through mastery learning
    d. through computer-assisted instruction

18. The roles for psychologists in business are BEST described as
    a. varied.
    b. limited to employee selection.
    c. management positions.
    d. consultant positions.

19. The study of the psychological reactions to our physical space is called _____ psychology.
    a. social
    b. environmental
    c. emotional
    d. health

20. In the office landscape format, offices are separated by
    a. walls.
    b. buildings.
    c. plants.
    d. partitions.

21. In terms of conviction rates, those who are _____ are convicted more often than those who are

    _____.
    a. rich; poor
    b. unattractive; attractive
    c. high-status; low-status
    d. attractive; unattractive

22. From 1930 to 1979, what population group had the highest number of executions?
    a. whites
    b. females
    c. Latin-Americans
    d. African-Americans

23. Studies of the debate format indicate that attorneys who speak _____ have an advantage.
    a. last
    b. first
    c. loudest
    d. softest

24. Traditionally, who is allowed to make the last statement to a jury?
    a. defendant
    b. witness
    c. prosecutor
    d. plaintiff

25. Who laid the foundation for educational testing?
    a. Sternberg
    b. Thorndike
    c. Binet
    d. Jefferson

26. Specialists employed by the school system to consult with teachers about special education programs are typically called
    a. guidance counselors.
    b. school psychologists.
    c. sociologists.
    d. social workers.

27. The mastery learning concept was proposed by
    a. Benjamin Bloom.
    b. Edward Thorndike.
    c. Thomas Jefferson.
    d. Alfred Binet.

28. Intelligent tutoring systems operate under the principles of
    a. mastery learning.
    b. puzzle groups.
    c. suite styles.
    d. participative management.

29. Testing aimed at establishing minimal educational criteria is the goal of _____ testing.
    a. reliable
    b. criterion-referenced
    c. standardized
    d. norm-referenced

30. Criterion-referenced testing establishes _____ that children must meet.
    a. practical criteria
    b. lofty goals
    c. multiple mastery levels
    d. normative databases

31. Handicapped children must receive educational and psychological assistance in circumstances that are as similar as possible to the environment of nonhandicapped children. In legal terms this is called the
    a. mastery learning environment.
    b. intelligent tutoring system.
    c. least restrictive environment.
    d. person x situation interaction.

32. Encouraging disabled children to participate in the regular classroom involves the process of
    a. mainstreaming.
    b. participatory classrooming.
    c. marketing.
    d. jigsaw classrooming.

Chapter 16 Answer Key

1. a	6. a	11. c	16. c	21. b	26. b	31. c
2. b	7. c	12. d	17. d	22. d	27. a	32. a
3. c	8. d	13. b	18. a	23. a	28. a	
4. d	9. a	14. a	19. b	24. c	29. b	
5. d	10. a	15. b	20. d	25. c	30. a	

Notes